The Sermon on the Mount

Fourth Edition 2006

Published by:
© Universal Life
The Inner Religion
P. O. Box 3549
Woodbridge, CT 06525
U S A

Licensed edition
translated from the original German title:
"Die Bergpredigt.
Leben nach dem Gesetz Gottes.
Danach streben die Urchristen im Universellen Leben."

From the Universal Life Series
with the consent of
© Verlag DAS WORT GmbH
im Universellen Leben
Max-Braun-Strasse 2
97828 Marktheidenfeld/Altfeld
Germany

Order No. S 008en

The German edition is the work of reference for all questions regarding the meaning of the contents.

ISBN 978-1-890841-42-3
ISBN 1-890841-42-0

Table of Contents

Introduction

Almost two thousand years ago, Jesus of Nazareth gave mankind the Sermon on the Mount. We can find essential parts of this teaching in the Bible (Mt. 5-7). The Sermon on the Mount contains the essence of the teaching of Jesus – key statements for a life according to the laws of God, tips for our relationship with our fellow men, with the animals, with nature. The one who puts these teachings into practice in his daily life will soon feel his life changing, that it becomes peaceful and positive.

But church leaders and politicians, especially those of the so-called Christian world, claim this teaching is utopian and cannot be put into practice.

Does this mean that Jesus of Nazareth was a utopian? Or was He the realist who could show us the way out of the maze of the human ego?

Christ, the Son of God, walked this earth as Jesus of Nazareth. His Redeemer-Spirit lives and is active in each one of us since the "It is finished" on Golgotha. Over the past two thousand years, He has spoken again and again through the mouth of prophets. Today, in this mighty time of radical change, He reveals Himself anew through His prophetess. He explains and deepens His teachings which He gave to humankind as Jesus of Nazareth. This is also the case in His great work of revelation "This Is My Word, A and Ω, the Gospel of Jesus – the

Christ-Revelation that true Christians the world over have come to know."

This work goes far beyond the content of the Bible; it gives us an overwhelming picture of what was, of what is and of what will be. In this revelation, Christ also gives mankind all-encompassing guidelines for a truly spiritual life in accordance with the divine laws. Thus, His words, spoken as Jesus of Nazareth, are fulfilled: "I have yet many things to say to you ..." (John 16:12). Building on an already existing gospel that is not part of the Bible, called the "Gospel of the Holy Twelve," Christ describes His living and working as Jesus of Nazareth in the book "This Is My Word." In particular, He points out to us how in today's time we can live in accordance with the laws of God, in accordance with the Ten Commandments and the Sermon on the Mount; and He gives us a preview of the future, of His Kingdom of Peace on earth.

The Sermon on the Mount of Jesus contains the essence of the path within, which Christ teaches today on all levels and in all detail in Universal Life and through His prophetic word. The Inner Path "Nearer, My God, to Thee" is the path of self-recognition and of overcoming one's human faults out of love for God. The person who successfully walks this path to selflessness, to equality, freedom, unity, brotherliness and justice receives the strength to fulfill more and more the Sermon on the Mount and the Ten Commandments in his daily life – even in business and commerce.

The intent of this book is to give all seeking people of our time an understanding of the Sermon on the Mount of Jesus – not only those parts documented in the Bible, but His teaching with explanations and deepenings that Christ has given to mankind in our time through His prophetic word. Beyond that, this book should give the reader insight into the depths of the work of revelation "This Is My Word, A and Ω, The Gospel of Jesus – The Christ-revelation that true Christians the world over have come to know."

In the latter work, Christ builds on the book "The Gospel of the Holy Twelve." However, since much of it is incomplete and sometimes falsely passed on, Christ explains and corrects this text today. Those passages which the Lord does not address more closely essentially agree with the truth of His life and work as Jesus of Nazareth. Beyond that, Christ deepens and expands the more important reports in the "The Gospel of Jesus." Thus, in the complete work "This Is My Word," mankind is now given the entire truth, all essential aspects of the life of Jesus and His teaching.

In the book "This Is My Word," one or more verses from "The Gospel of the Holy Twelve" are followed by the words with which Christ explained, corrected and deepened the individual passages in 1989. This form was maintained while rendering the excerpts at hand. However, titles are used to subdivide the text and organize it in a clear way.

The words of Christ to the future inhabitants of His Kingdom of Peace about the life and activities of the pioneers of this kingdom are not repeated in the revelation text of the Sermon on the Mount from "This Is My Word," because these statements do not concern the text of the Sermon on the Mount.

This book contains the Twelve Commandments of Jesus that He has now given to mankind anew in His work of revelation "This Is My Word," (Chap. 46:7-21). In essence, they are the Ten Commandments that God revealed through Moses and that Jesus of Nazareth expanded for His Kingdom of Peace in coming on earth.

The following information will also be important for the reader who wants to actualize in his life the commandments of the Sermon on the Mount of Jesus. After revealing the complete content of His Sermon on the Mount and the revelation of the path to God in the innermost being of every person, Christ revealed in 1991 the highest law to us, the Absolute Law, in His work, "The Great Cosmic Teachings of Jesus of Nazareth to His Apostles and Disciples Who Could Understand Them. The Life of True God-filled Men." It is the law of the heavens, given as further help to all those who have set out to become pure in heart again through the fulfillment of the laws of God.

God gave and gives. He does not ask whether a person recognizes His word, the word of God, and lives accordingly. Each one can examine and decide for himself. May the one who can grasp it, grasp it.

The Sermon on the Mount

The Beatitudes

1. When Jesus saw the multitudes, He went on a mountain. And when He had sat down, the twelve came to Him. He looked up at His disciples, saying:

2. Blessed in the spirit are the poor, for theirs is the Kingdom of Heaven. Blessed are those who grieve, for they shall be comforted. Blessed are the meek, for they will possess the earth. Blessed are those who hunger and thirst for righteousness, for they shall be satisfied.

3. Blessed are the merciful, for they will attain mercy. Blessed are the pure in heart, for they will behold God. Blessed are the peacemakers, for they will be called children of God. Blessed are those who are persecuted for righteousness' sake, for theirs is the Kingdom of God.

4. Blessed are you, when men will hate you and exclude you from their company and speak all sorts of evil against you and outlaw your names, for the sake of the Son of Man. Rejoice in that day and leap with joy, for behold, your reward is great in heaven. For their forefathers did the same to the prophets. (Chap. 25:1-4)

Christ explains, corrects
and deepens the word:

The Sermon on the Mount is the Inner Path to the heart of God, which leads to perfection.

The blessed ones will behold the Christ and will possess the earth with Me, the Christ, in all meekness and humility. Happy the one who beholds the glory of the Father-Mother-God in all things! He has become the living example for many.

I guide My own to the recognition of the truth.

The one who is of the truth hears My voice, because he is the truth, and thus hears and perceives the truth, as well.

The blessed ones are fearless and joyful; for they perceive and hear what those do not see and hear, who still hide behind their human ego, holding on to it with utmost effort so that they are not recognized.

However, the blessed ones look into the dungeon of the human ego and recognize the deepest hidden thoughts of their fellow men. With the strength of their light-filled consciousness, they shine into it and call out to their fellow men:

"Blessed in the spirit are the poor, for theirs is the Kingdom of Heaven!"

The words "the poor" do not mean material poverty. It is not this that brings bliss in the spirit, but the devotion to God, from which the person fulfills all these things that are the will of God. This is the inner wealth.

The words "the poor" mean all those who do not strive for personal possessions and do not hoard goods. Their thinking and striving aims at the community life in which they administer the goods that God has given to everyone in a lawful way. They do not set their minds and aspire to having worldly things. They serve the common good and extend their arms to God and consciously walk the path to the Inner Life. Their goal is the Kingdom of God in their inner being, which they want to proclaim and bring to all people who are of good will. Their inner wealth is the life in God, a life for God and for their neighbor. They live the commandment "pray and work."

They strive toward the Spirit of God and receive from God what they need for their earthly life and beyond that. They are the blessed in the Spirit of God.

"Blessed are those who grieve, for they shall be comforted."

The grief of man does not come from God; it is either the grieving one who himself has caused it, or, in the realm of the souls, his soul has taken over a part of the debt of a brother or sister soul to pay off that debt in an earthly existence, so that the brother or sister soul can go into higher spheres of Inner Life.

God's mercy will be granted to the one who bears his grief without accusing his neighbor, recognizing his faults and weaknesses in the grief, repenting of them, asking for forgiveness and forgiving. For God, the Eternal, wants to comfort His children and to take away from them what is not good and beneficial for their soul. For when the grief leaves the soul, that is, when the causes that became effective in the soul are settled, a person finds his way closer to God.

"Bear your grief" means: Do not complain about it; do not accuse God or your neighbor. In your grief, find the sinful behavior that led to it.

Repent, forgive and ask for forgiveness, and no longer do what you have recognized as sin. Then the debt of the soul can be erased by God and you receive increased strength, love and wisdom from Him.

If you meet a grieving and sorely afflicted person and he asks you for help, then support him and help him as far as it is possible for you and as far as it is good for his soul. And when you see that your neighbor thankfully accepts the help and builds himself up with it, then give him even more, if it is possible for you.

However, you who give help, do it selflessly. If you do it only as an external obligation, you will receive no spiritual reward – and you will render no service to the soul of the person who is suffering and is sorely afflicted, but only to his body, to the vehicle of the soul.

"Blessed are the meek, for they will possess the earth."

Meekness, humility, love and kindness go hand in hand. The one who has become selfless love is also meek, humble and kind. He is filled with wisdom and strength.

People in My Spirit, the selflessly loving ones, will possess the earth. Oh see, the path to the heart of God is the path into the heart of selfless love. The peace of God flows out of selfless love.

The people who journey toward the heart of God and the people who already live in God work for the New Era, by teaching all willing people the path to God. In this way, they take possession of the earth more and more in My Spirit.

"Blessed are those who hunger and thirst for righteousness, for they shall be satisfied."

The one who hungers and thirsts for the righteousness of God is a seeker of truth, who longs for the life in and with God. He shall be satisfied.

My brother, My sister, you, who long for righteousness, for the life in and with God, take heart and raise yourself out of the sinful human ego! Rejoice, for the time has come in which the Kingdom of God draws closer to those people who endeavor to keep the commandments of life.

Behold, I, your Redeemer, Am the truth in you. And so, in you, I Am the way, the truth and the life.

The truth is the law of love and of life. In the Ten Commandments, which are excerpts from the all-encompassing law of God, you find the retentive phrases for the path to the truth. Keep the Ten Commandments and you will draw ever more onto the path of the Sermon on the Mount, in which the path to the truth is fundamentally worked out.

The path to the truth is the path to the heart of God, to the eternal life, which is selfless love. The Sermon on the Mount is the pathway into the Kingdom of God, into the laws for the Kingdom of Peace of Jesus Christ. When you delve deeper into them and fulfill them, you attain divine wisdom.

Recognize that no one should hunger or thirst for righteousness. Take the first step toward the kingdom of love by first being righteous to yourself. Practice a positive way of living and thinking and you will very gradually become a righteous person. Then you will bring the righteousness of God into this world; and you will also represent this because you fulfill the will of God, the Lord, out of His love and wisdom.

Recognize: The time is near when what was prophesied takes place. The lion will lie by the lamb, because the people have gained victory over themselves – through Me, their Redeemer. They will form a great family in God and will live in unity with all animals and with all of nature.

Be glad, for the Kingdom of God has drawn close – and, with the Kingdom of God, I, too, your Redeemer and bringer of peace, the ruler of the Kingdom of Peace, of the World Kingdom of Jesus Christ.

"Blessed are the merciful, for they will attain mercy."

The mercy of God corresponds to the gentleness and kindness of God and is, for all souls, the gate to the completion of life. The people who have unfolded in their souls all the seven basic forces of life – the law, from Order to Mercy – through Me, the Christ, who lives in the Father-Mother-God, will, as pure spirit beings, again enter selfless love through the gate of mercy. They will go into the Kingdom of God, the heavens, and will live in peace. The seventh basic force, the Mercy – called kindness and gentleness in the Spirit of God – is the gate to the eternal Being. All people who practice being merciful will also attain mercy and will stand by those who are on their inner way to mercy.

Recognize: The path to the heart of God is the path of the individual in community with those of like mind. For God is unity, and unity in God is community in and with God and with one's neighbor.

The one who has taken the first steps on the path to completion will fulfill the commandment of unity: One for all, Christ – and all for One, Christ.

As revealed, the Sermon on the Mount is the path of evolution toward the Inner Life. All those who are further ahead on this path of unfoldment toward the heart of God help, in turn, those who are only at the beginning of the path. In and over all, shines the Christ, who I Am.

"Blessed are the pure in heart, for they will behold God."

The pure heart is the pure soul that has raised itself again to be an absolute spirit being through Me, the Christ in the Father-Mother-God.

The pure souls that have again become beings of the heavens are then the image of the eternal Father once more, and behold the Eternal again, face to face. At the same time, they see, live and hear the law of the eternal Father, because they have again become spirit of His Spirit – the eternal law, itself.

As long as people and souls still have to listen for the Spirit of God in themselves, they are not yet spirit of His Spirit; they are not yet the law of love and of life, itself.

However, the one who has again become the law of love and life beholds the eternal Father face to face and is in constant conscious communication with Him. He also perceives the law of God, the life from God, as a whole, because he himself is the life and the love, and moves in them. Whoever moves in the Absolute Law of God has also opened it completely – from order all the way to mercy. All the seven basic powers of infinity serve him, because he is in absolute unity and harmony with all Being.

"Blessed are the peacemakers, for they will be called children of God."

According to their meaning, these words are saying: Blessed are those who keep peace. They will also bring true peace to this earth, because they have become peaceful in themselves. They are consciously the children of God.

"Blessed are those who suffer persecution for righteousness' sake, for theirs is the Kingdom of God."

Recognize: The one who followed Me was not respected by the worldlings, because I, too, as Jesus, was held in disdain by them. At all times, people who entered into the true following of the Nazarene had to endure and suffer much.

The Calls of Woe

5. Woe unto you who are rich! For you have received your consolation in this life. Woe unto you who are sated, for you will hunger. Woe unto you who laugh now, for you will mourn and weep. Woe unto you when all men speak well of you, for so did their forefathers with the false prophets. (Chap. 25:5)

Christ explains, corrects
and deepens the word:

"Woe unto you who are rich, for you have received your consolation in this life."

People who look upon their wealth as their property are poor in spirit. Many who are rich in earthly goods were given in the cradle the spiritual task for their earthly life, to be an example to those rich people who tie themselves to their wealth with hardened, relentless hearts and whose sole thinking and striving consists in increasing this wealth for themselves. A person who is rich in earthly goods and has recognized that his wealth is a gift – which he has received from God only to bring it into the great whole for the well-being of everyone and to administer it in the right way for all – is the one who actualizes the law of equality, freedom, unity and brotherhood. He contributes as a selfless giver, so that the poor do not live in privation and the rich in luxury.

In this way, a balance will gradually be established, an upper middle class for all those who are willing to selflessly fulfill the law "pray and work." Thus grows very gradually the true humanity of a community whose members do not collect personal earthly riches, but rather consider everything to be common property given to them by God.

If a rich person considers money and property as his own and is esteemed in the world because of his wealth, then – as the effect of his causes – he will live in poor countries in subsequent earthly lives and there, he will beg for the bread that, as a rich man, he once denied the poor. This will happen as long as such incarnations are still possible.

The soul of such a rich person will also find no rest in the spheres of purification. The souls that are poor in light and had to endure suffering and hunger in the earthly garment because of him will recognize him again as the one who denied them what could have helped them out of the entanglement of the human ego. Many will accuse him and then his soul itself will feel how they suffered and hungered. In this way, a soul that was rich and esteemed as a human being in the earthly garment may suffer great need; this need is far greater than if it would have had to beg for bread in the earthly garment.

Recognize that according to the laws of the Eternal, everyone who selflessly keeps the commandment "pray and work" is due the same; for God gives everyone what he needs and beyond that. However, as long as this commandment is not kept by all people, there will be the so-called rich on earth. It is their task to distribute their accumulated wealth and to live just as those who selflessly fulfill the commandment "pray and work." If, in this way, they think of the welfare of all and not of their own, the inner wealth will gradually turn without and no person will hunger or live in want.

Woe to you, you rich ones, you who call your money and property your own and make your neighbor work so that your wealth may increase! I say to you, that you will not behold the throne of God, but will continue to live where God's feet are – on earth, in earthly garments over and over, as long as this is still possible. Even if you promote social service establishments, but are yourselves so much wealthier than those who are thereby supported, you are nevertheless servile to the satan of the senses, that wants the differences between rich and poor.

Through these differences, power and subservience, envy and hatred emerge. These give rise to dispute and war. For this reason, even though every now and then they think of the social good, those who cling to their wealth serve the satan of the senses and act against the law of life: against equality, freedom, unity and brotherliness.

According to the law of life, the person who considers money and property as his own and hoards them for himself, instead of letting these material energies flow, is a thief, for he denies his neighbors a part of their spiritual heritage. For everything is energy. The one who ties it up through "me" and "mine" acts against the law, which is flowing energy.

"Woe unto you who are sated, for you will hunger."

The wealthy, sated man who fills only "his" barns is empty of heart. He knows only the mine and thine. His senses and thoughts revolve around "my" property, "my" possessions, "my" bread, "my" food. "All this belongs to me" – this is his world. Such a person will one day hunger and live in want until he realizes that everything is the Being; everything belongs to God and to all people who strive to do the works of God: to fulfill selfless love and the law of life for the earth, "pray and work."

People who speak only of mine and thine are poor in light, and already in this incarnation are preparing another sojourn on earth or a long pilgrimage in the realm of the souls and, in both cases, in the garment of a beggar.

The soul that is dazzled by material things is unconsciously hungering for light, because it is poor in light. It compulsively tries to compensate for this with outer things, such as earthly wealth, greed, gluttony, alcoholism or other cravings and pleasures. It is insatiable.

"Woe unto you who laugh now, for you will mourn and weep."

The one who laughs and mocks his neighbor will one day be very sad and will cry over himself – because he failed to acknowledge those whom he ridiculed and mocked. He will have to recognize that, in the end, he had laughed at himself; he had scorned and ridiculed himself. For the one who judges and condemns his neighbor, who laughs at him, who scorns and ridicules him, judges, condemns, laughs at, scorns and ridicules Me, the Christ.

Recognize that whoever sins against the least of My brothers sins against the law of life and will have to suffer from this. At the same time, he has tied himself to the one he held in disdain. Therefore, be on your guard and practice self-control. It is not what enters through your mouth that soils your soul, rather it is what goes out from your mouth that burdens soul and person.

"Woe unto you when all men speak well of you, for so did their forefathers with the false prophets."

If you flatter your fellow man, so that he praise you and hold you in esteem, then you are like the counterfeiters who, for the sake of their own advantage, pay with false money.

It was and is similar with the false prophets, as well. They were and are esteemed by the people because they flattered the people and because those of high standing among the people were in league with them, having promised themselves personal profit and gain through this.

Recognize, you people in the Kingdom of Peace, that in the sinful world many righteous prophets and enlightened men and women, as well, were slandered and perecuted by the rich and the powerful of this world, by church leaders and their adherents, and many of them were tortured and killed. At all times, the satanic used as tools those who wanted to keep and increase their earthly wealth for themselves, who strove for power and those who were servile to the rich and powerful, as well.

You should know this, so that you can understand why the old, sinful world perished in such a terrible way.

In addition, false prophets were also those who may very well have preached the gospel of love, but themselves did not live accordingly. And they were also all those who called themselves "Christian" and behaved in an unchristian way in their life. They were often lauded for their eloquence and were honored and praised because of their wealth and prestige.

Oh see, nevertheless and over the course of time, all true prophets and enlightened ones contributed to the fact that the crystal of Inner Life, with its many facets of eternal truth, sparkled and shone more and more. In this way, the Kingdom of God on earth was very gradually built up.

It is up to you, dear brothers and sisters in the Kingdom of Peace, to cherish, guard and preserve this now perfect, sparkling and shining crystal, the Inner Life, like a precious flower. It is the law of love and wisdom of God, His order, His will, His wisdom, His earnestness, His kindness, His infinite love-radiation, and His gentleness.

You Are the Salt of the Earth

6. You are the salt of the earth; for every sacrifice must be salted with salt, but if the salt has lost its taste, with what shall one salt? Henceforth, it is good for nothing, but to be poured out and trodden underfoot. (Chap. 25:6)

Christ explains, corrects
and deepens the word:

The righteous are the salt of the earth.

They will repeatedly point out the deplorable state of affairs of this world and touch upon the sore points of sin. For much damage has been and is being done in this still sinful world – and many people became victims for the sake of the gospel.

The righteous who became victims shall be vindicated by righteous men and women, for everything shall be made manifest through the salt of the earth. Now, in this time of radical change from the old sinful world to the New Era, the Era of Light, the righteous will bring injustice to light and will cause it to become evident, so that those who have done wrong may recognize themselves and atone for it.

However, you righteous ones, who are the salt of the earth, beware that the salt does not lose its taste, that you, therefore, remain in righteousness and do not let yourselves be led astray. For who shall bring righteousness into this world, and who shall point out the deplorable state of affairs and the sins that people have created? Surely, only those who know My name and are recorded in the book of the lamb.

The one who no longer is salt of the earth falls among those who have abused and are abusing My name for their own purposes and who have persecuted, slandered and killed the righteous.

When the salt of the earth loses its taste and the person disregards his neighbor, he will succumb to his own causes; figuratively speaking, he will trample himself underfoot. His unexpiated causes will then cause illness, infirmity and grief. The light-poor soul will live in need and will feel on its own soul body what it has caused to its neighbor.

You Are the Light of the World

7. You are the light of the world. The city that is built on a hill cannot be concealed. Neither does one light a candle and put it under a bushel, but on a candlestick; and it gives light to all who are in the house. Let your light so shine before the people, that they may see your good works and praise your Father who is in heaven. (Chap. 25:7)

Christ explains, corrects
and deepens the word:

I Am the light of the world.

In the mighty turn of time, more and more hearts were kindled by My light. The people recognized the eternal truth in My words. Ever more people followed the Inner Path and accepted the gift of life, the teachings and lessons from the eternal truth, in order to draw closer to God, the eternal Being.

Many men and women became My faithful ones, for they fulfilled the will of God. They became brothers and sisters in My Spirit and became the pioneers for the New Era, who laid the foundation of the Kingdom of God on earth and began to build on it.

8. You should not think that I Am come to destroy the law or the prophets; I Am not come to destroy, but to fulfill. For verily, I say to you: Till heaven and earth pass away, not the smallest letter nor one dot will pass away from the law or the prophets until all that is fulfilled. But behold, One greater than Moses is here, and He will give you the higher law, even the perfect law, and you shall obey this law. (Chap. 25:8)

Christ explains, corrects
and deepens the word:

As Jesus of Nazareth, I taught parts of the perfect law, of the Absolute Law, to the men and women who followed Me and all those who listened to Me. I also explained to them that the absolute law of love shines into the law of sowing and reaping; for the Spirit is omnipresent and is also active in the law of sowing and reaping, the law of the Fall.

Through Me as Jesus of Nazareth, the incarnated Christ, and through all other true prophets of God that followed, the Eternal taught and admonished His children in the imperfect planes that the law of the Fall, the law of sowing and reaping, is constantly active. The one who does not stop and think it over and does not turn back in time will have to bear his causes as effects. The Eternal was and is making every effort, also in today's time [1989], to lead His human children and all souls to His heart, to the law of eternal love, before the harvest – the effects of the causes created by them – falls upon them. The Eternal led and leads them to self-recognition through Me, Christ. He gave and gives them the strength to clear up what they recognized and recognize as a sin and shortcoming.

In Jesus of Nazareth, the Christ, who I Am, came to this earth, into this world, to teach, as the Son of Man, the eternal law to the people and to live it as an example. This was done so that the people would recognize the path to the eternal Father and fulfill His law – and thus be able to again enter the eternal homes that He keeps ready for all His children.

The people who followed Me during My lifetime on earth and who actualized the eternal laws were My true followers.

In the generations that followed, there existed a Christianity and a sham Christianity: the true followers who freely followed Me, the Christ, by keeping the laws of the Sermon on the Mount – and the sham Christians who just talked about Me, the Christ, but acted against the laws. In addition, there was the so-called coerced following of Christ: This resulted from the forced Christianization of the masses carried out by the churches.

Recognize: There is no coercion in the eternal law. God, the Eternal, has given all His children free will. The one who freely decides has the strength, through his free decision, for what characterizes true Christianity:

equality, freedom, unity, brotherliness and justice. All coercion comes from the law of sowing and reaping, also called the law of the Fall. We are called to freely choose our spiritual path. I, Christ, offered and offer the path to the heart of God, but I force no person to walk it. Whoever forces his neighbor, himself lives under the coercion of the law of the Fall and personifies the Fall-thought.

Several so-called Christian denominations force their faithful into baptism with water. Even little children whose free will is not yet developed and who therefore cannot yet decide for themselves are forced, through baptism by water, into membership of a church and thereby induced to participate in its other rituals.

This is an infringement on the individual's free will and, a forced Christianization, so to speak. These are the things that take place under the law of the Fall.

People who do not freely accept and receive Me, Christ, out of the deepest inner conviction, often have great difficulties in correctly understanding and accepting the Ten Commandments, the excerpts from the eternal law. This is because these have been pushed into the background through many externalizations, dogmatic ceremonies, rites, customs and cults. Within the denominations, these externalizations take on a main role; yet, they have nothing in common with inner Christianity, the inner religion, but stemmed, in part, directly from the times of polytheism and idolatry, and thus, from the region of the Fall-planes.

Only when people freely break away from the dogmas and rigid ceremonies that have been forced upon them, from rites and cults, as well as from their own concepts of God, can they gradually be guided into their inner being, into their true being. There, in their inner being, they then find themselves as true beings in God and as inhabitants of the Kingdom of God, which is within, in every person. This Inner Life is the true religion, the inner religion.

Recognize: The eternal, all-embracing, universal law, the law of the heavens, is irrevocable. It is the law of all pure Being. The law of sowing and reaping emerged through the Fall and can be dissolved only through the actualization of the eternal laws. However, it cannot be evaded. The law of sowing and reaping remains active in each soul, until the sins are recognized, cleared up, atoned for and surrendered to Me, the Christ of God. The Fall-law in the soul is then cancelled. Furthermore, the soul is then freed of its impurity for the most part. It again becomes the pure being in God that lives the Absolute Law, since it strives again toward the absolute, all-ruling law of love and of life.

The law of sowing and reaping holds true until everything unlawful is settled and transformed into positive energy, and every being again lives in God, out of which it came forth. In the same degree to which all beings from God have again been received into the heart of God, into the Absolute Law, will all purification planes – all part-material and material planes, including the earth – transform into cosmic energy and again vibrate in the Absolute Law. Then the Fall-law has been abolished, and God's love is all-prevailing and consciously in all Being, in every being.

Not one "dot" will be removed from the eternal law, which the true prophets brought before and after Me, and which I, as Jesus of Nazareth, lived as an example.

When it says "not the smallest letter," then it is referring to a single aspect of the eternal truth, not the letter and the word of human beings as such. Human words are often only symbols that conceal what is deep within. Only when a person is able to feel into the language of symbols does he recognize the truth and the meaning of life, which lies deeply hidden in human words.

"The higher law" is the step into the perfect law. This will be taught – to the mostly pure beings that have come from earth and the soul realms – in the preparation planes, which are situated before the gate to heaven. The higher law is the last level of instruction before the gate to heaven. It shows the mostly pure beings how the lawful radiation is reactivated in the spirit body, so that it can be applied in infinity.

As Jesus of Nazareth, I taught parts of the perfect law, the Absolute Law. The whole truth still had to remain concealed from the people in those days, because they were still too attached to their belief in gods and too oriented toward the various trends of belief of that time. For that reason, I spoke in the following sense: When the time has come, I, the Spirit of truth, will lead you into all truth.

On the hill of Golgotha – this means, the place of the skulls – I was crucified by the Romans, because the Jewish people had not accepted and received Me as the Messiah. Although I preached, taught, healed and gave many signs of My deity up and down the valley of the Jordan, the stubborn Jewish people remained submissive to the ministers of the temple, thus becoming partly responsible for the death of Jesus of Nazareth.

With the words that mean "It is finished," the Redeemer-Spark entered all burdened and fallen souls. Through this, I became and Am the Redeemer of all men and souls.

As the Christ of God, I acted and continue to act. In all generations up to the present time [1989], I gave and give My revelations through true instruments of God, through people whose souls are mostly purified.

During this mighty turn of time, in which the Era of Light draws ever closer to man, I teach the eternal law in all its facets, and ever more people walk the path within, to the love of God.

Now the time is come, which I announced as Jesus of Nazareth. "Today you are not yet able to bear it, that is, to grasp it; yet "when the Spirit of truth comes, He will guide you into all truth." Now, in spirit, I Am among My own, the faithful pilgrims to the eternal Being, to the consciousness of My Father; and I teach them the absolute, eternal law, so that those, too, who will live in the Kingdom of Peace may fulfill it and thereby live in Me and I through them.

My words are life; they are the eternal law. They are preserved in the pilgrims to the eternal life and in many written records as well – as it is with this book – for the Kingdom of Peace of Jesus Christ.

Recognize: Only the eternal law of love makes people free – not the law of sowing and reaping. This brings them only suffering, illness, misery and infirmity.

Keep the Commandments – Only Then Teach

9. The one who breaks one of these commandments, which He gives and teaches the people to do the same, will be called the least in the Kingdom of Heaven. But the one who keeps and teaches them, the same will be called great in the Kingdom of Heaven. (Chap. 25:9)

Christ explains, corrects
and deepens the word:

The Ten Commandments that God gave to His human children through Moses are excerpts from the eternal law of life and of love. Whoever violates these commandments, who only teaches them to his fellow man but does not keep them himself, is a false teacher. He sins against the Holy Spirit. This is the greatest sin. This counterfeiter uses the love of God, the law of life, for his own purpose. Thereby, he misuses the eternal law. Every misuse is thievery; and every thief is a hunted and hounded person who, sooner or later, is caught and convicted by his own deeds, by his own causes. For God is a just God; everything will be revealed through Him, the good as well as the less good and the evil.

However, the one who keeps the law of love and of life, that is, who fulfills it in his daily life, and teaches the people what he himself has actualized is a true spiritual teacher. He offers the bread of the heavens to the people and will thus satisfy many. The one who gives out of his own fulfillment is filled by divine wisdom and strength and, when the time has come, will shine like a star in heaven. For the God-filled person draws from the stream of salvation and gives selflessly to those who hunger and thirst for righteousness.

Recognize: Through such righteous men and women, the eternal law of love and of life comes into this world. And so, the one who keeps and teaches the eternal law will be called great in the Kingdom of Heaven; this means that he will harvest a rich reward in heaven.

Live According to Your Recognition

10. Verily, those who believe and obey will save their souls, and those who do not obey will lose them. For I say to you: If your righteousness is not greater than that of the scribes and Pharisees, you will not enter the Kingdom of Heaven. (Chap. 25:10)

Christ explains, corrects
and deepens the word:

The statement, "... those who believe and obey will save their souls, and those who do not obey will lose them" means that the one who believes and follows the laws of God will deliver his soul from the wheel of reincarnation, which will continue to draw him into the flesh until he has atoned for everything that repeatedly drew him into incarnation.

Recognize: The mere belief in the law of life is not enough. Only the belief in the life and the actualization of the laws of life lead man and soul out of the wheel of reincarnation.

Whoever does not keep the laws of God betrays God and sells his soul to the darkness. Through this, he covers the light of his soul, his true life. This person then lives in sin and his soul lives in the slumber of this world. The law of incarnation, the wheel of reincarnation that draws the soul into incarnation, will still be in effect for quite a considerable length of time, so that the incarnated soul may recognize that it is not of this world, but is in the earthly garment to discard what is human – and to uncover what is divine: its true, eternal life.

Not all who know the written characters interpret them only literally, but do so according to the meaning. For this reason, it should say: If your righteousness is not greater than that of the many scribes – who pretend to be righteous and teach My law, but do not keep it themselves – you will not enter the Kingdom of Heaven.

Therefore, do not tie yourselves to the opinions and views of people. Actualize what you have recognized from the law of life; then you will recognize the continuing steps to higher spiritual principles.

Recognize that the justice of God is the love and wisdom of God. The one who does not bring them to unfoldment in himself does not radiate them; he neither perceives the depth of eternal Being nor fathoms his true life. His earthly life is in a state of vegetation and in this state he passes by the true life. On this side of life as well as in the beyond, he is the spiritually dead one. Neither in this earthly existence nor in the life beyond does he have the right orientation, because he did not live according to the laws of life. He is not wise, but only passes on the knowledge he has stored. Thus, he becomes a follower of sin and finally, a sinner. He acts against the eternal law and in this way falls deeper and deeper into the law of sowing and reaping.

Reconcile with Your Neighbor

11. Therefore, when you offer your gift on the altar and remember that your brother has something against you, leave your gift before the altar, go there first and reconcile with your brother, and then come and offer your gift. (Chap. 25:11)

Christ explains, corrects
and deepens the word:

If you want to devote your life to Me, the Christ, and surrender your faults and sins to Me, and you recognize that you have not yet reconciled with your neighbor, then leave your sin lying before the inner altar for the moment. Go to your neighbor and reconcile with him – and, if you no longer want to do the same or similar thing that led to the sin, then place your sin upon the altar. The altar is in the innermost part of your temple of flesh and bone. The Spirit of love and life will then transform the sin into strength and life. For you will attain liberation from that which you freely, willingly and without pressure surrender to Me, thus no longer doing the same or similar thing. Your soul will then increasingly receive the light from Me.

Take heed of the following lawful principle: When you have sinned against your neighbor exclusively in thoughts, through unloving, envious, revengeful, jealous or hate-filled thoughts, then do not go to him to talk about it. Know that your neighbor does not know your world of thoughts. If you let it be manifest in words, he will think about it. Come solely to Me, the Christ, who I Am in your inner being, and repent of your thoughts. At the same time, send positive, selfless thoughts to the soul of your neighbor, thoughts of asking for forgiveness and of inner unity. Then I will undo what was caused in thoughts. And if you no longer think the same or similar thing, then it is already forgiven you.

Recognize: If you speak to your neighbor of your human thoughts, you might possibly stir up in him some human aspect that is just in the process of transformation. It could then break out once again in your neighbor. He then begins to think and speak negatively again, burdening himself anew.

The law says that through your wrong behavior not only the one who is stimulated to think about it again burdens himself, but you, too, burden yourself when you express your thoughts and, through this, activate in your neighbor the human aspects that were in the process of transformation.

However, if unlawful things leave your mouth in that you accuse and insult your neighbor and speak ill of him – even if he hears it from a second or third party – then go to him and ask him for forgiveness. If he forgives you, so does the eternal heavenly Father in Me, the Christ, also forgive you. But if he does not forgive you, then your heavenly Father in Me, the Christ, will not be able to forgive you either. However, the love of the Father-Mother-God will touch the still rigid heart more and more, so that the person will sooner think things over and forgive you, and so that God in Me, the Christ, can also forgive you; then all that was once against the law is annulled and transformed.

Beware of your own tongue! For the unlawful things that leave your mouth can do much greater harm to your neighbor and to yourself than your thoughts, which you recognize in time and surrender to Me, the Christ in you, – before they have taken effect.

Recognize another principle of the law: You cannot see or hear thoughts – and yet they are there. They vibrate in the atmosphere and can influence the one who thinks the same or like things. If you surrender them to Me, in time, they are cancelled – unless the soul of your neighbor has already registered them. Then, you will be guided in such a way that you will be able to do good to the person of whom you thought negatively. And if you do good selflessly, without expressing your earlier thoughts, then what you unlawfully thought about your neighbor and which he already had absorbed into his soul will be erased. And what your soul had radiated is erased in you, as well.

Forgive – and Ask for Forgiveness

12. Reach agreement with your adversary quickly, while you are still on your way with him, lest one day your adversary hand you over to the judge, and the judge hand you over to the guard, and you will not come out until you have paid the last penny. (Chap. 25:12)

Christ explains, corrects
and deepens the word:

"Reach agreement with your adversary quickly, while you are still on your way with him" means: Do not let the sin that you committed against your neighbor linger. Clear it up as quickly as possible, for he is still with you on your path through life in an earthly existence. If his soul has left the earth, you may have to wait until you can meet him again and ask him for forgiveness.

Recognize: The judge is the law of sowing and reaping. If it becomes effective, the person will not come out from under it until he has paid the "last penny" – that is, until everything that he caused and did not repent of in time is atoned.

For this reason, use the chance to ask your neighbor for forgiveness and to forgive him as long as you are still on your way, walking over the earth with him, and the sin has not yet engraved itself in the soul and become a cause. The one who does not forgive or ask for forgiveness has to bear the effect until he has "paid the last penny."

Therefore, become one with your neighbor as quickly as possible. If the causes – for example, quarrel, resentment or envy – have already taken root in your soul, and if the same has also taken place in the neighbor whom you are against, then it is possible that your neighbor will not forgive you so quickly – not even when you have recognized your sin and repented. For the guilt complex may have hardened in his soul through the same or similar way of thinking that you had triggered in him. Through your sinful behavior that was nurtured over a longer period of time, he also nursed a grudge against you in his soul – and, like you, he has thus created an extensive and unlawful energy field, a guilt complex, that now has to be worked on by both of you. Clearing this up can still take place during this earthly existence or even later in the realms of the souls or in further incarnations.

Recognize that before a blow of fate strikes a person, he is admonished by the Spirit of life, which is also the life of the soul, and by his guardian spirit or by people, as well. The admonishments from the Spirit are the finest sensations that flow from the soul or that the guardian spirit lets flow into the person's world of sensations or thoughts. They admonish the person to change his way of thinking or to clear up what he has caused. The eternal Spirit of life and the guardian spirit may also stimulate people to go to the one who is on the verge of being struck by a blow of fate. They will approach the person concerned and enter a conversation that will spontaneously refer to the matter in question. From this conversation, the cause of the looming fate may be recognized and cleared up.

And so, you can see that the eternal light gives admonishments and indications in manifold ways and means – both to your neighbor with whom you have created causes, as well as to you, yourselves.

And through impulses by way of the day's events, a person is admonished in time, before what was caused by him breaks in over him as fate.

Anyone who takes such hints seriously and clears up the sins he recognized, by repenting, forgiving, asking for forgiveness and making amends, need not bear what was caused by him. If the sin is great, then it is possible that he will have to bear a part of what wanted to break out of the soul, but not all of it. However, the one who overlooks and fails to heed all the admonishments, because he has numbed himself with human things, will have to bear his self-created causes until "the last penny is paid."

Love Your Enemies

13. You have heard that it has been said: You shall love your neighbor and hate your enemy. But I say to you who listen: Love your enemies, do good to those who hate you. (Chap. 25:13)

Christ explains, corrects
and deepens the word:

The commandment of life reads, "Love your enemies, do good to those who hate you."

Every person should see his neighbor, his brother and sister, in each of his fellow men. Even in your seeming enemy, you should recognize your neighbor and strive to love him selflessly.

The seeming enemy can even be a good mirror for your self-recognition when you become upset because of the hostility, which may have many faces; for when something about your neighbor upsets you, the same or similar thing is in you, as well.

However, if you are able to forgive your neighbor, who has blamed and accused you, without being unduly agitated, no correspondence is in you; that is, you do not have the same or similar thing in you and thus, no resonance for this in your soul. It is possible that, in a former life, you already cleared up and atoned what you were accused of – or even that you never built it up in your soul. Then, it was only in the soul of the one who thought and spoke against you and accused you. Therefore, if no emotion reverberates in you, if no echo comes from your soul, then you were a mirror for him. Whether he looks into this mirror for his human ego or not – leave that to God and to him, His child.

Recognize: Even the mere sight of you stirs his conscience and reflects to him that, for example, he once thought and spoke unlawfully about you. Now he has the chance to clear it up. If he does this, by repenting and henceforth no longer thinking or doing the same or similar thing, then it is removed, that is, transformed, in his soul. Only then will he see you with the eyes of inner light.

A sign that the unlawful has been transformed into the positive in a soul is the good will and understanding toward one's neighbor.

Bless Those Who Curse You

14. Bless those who curse you and pray for those who abuse you out of wickedness, so that you may be children of your Father who is in heaven and who lets the sun rise on the evil and the good and sends rain on the just and the unjust. (Chap. 25:14)

Christ explains, corrects
and deepens the word:

The one who keeps these commandments is just toward his fellow man and, through a life in God, he will guide many people to the life in God. God does not punish and chastise His children. This is already said by the words, "... who lets the sun rise on the evil and the good and sends rain on the just and the unjust."

God is the giver of life, because He is the life, Himself. From the eternal law of life, God gave human beings the free will to decide freely for or against Him. Whoever is for Him keeps the eternal laws of love and of life and will also receive the gifts of love and of life from the eternal law. The one who feels, thinks and acts against the eternal law receives what he has sown, that is, what he felt, thought, spoke and did.

Therefore, everyone receives what he himself has sown. The one who sows good seed, that is, who fulfills the laws of God, will also reap good fruits. The one who sows human seeds, which he brings into the field of his soul as human sensations, thoughts, words and deeds, will also harvest the corresponding fruits.

From this, you can see that God does not intervene in the will of man. He is the giver, helper, admonisher, leader and protector of those who endeavor to do His will, because they turn to Him. The one who turns away from Him, by creating his own human law, will also be controlled by his own human "ego-law."

And so, God does not interfere in the law of sowing and reaping. In manifold ways, God reaches out to His children; and those who sincerely pray to Him from their heart and fulfill what I, the Christ in God, My Father, have commanded them – to love one another selflessly – are in God, and God is active through them.

Accept Your Neighbor in Your Heart

15. For if you love those who love you, what reward will you have? For sinners also love those who love them. And if you do good to those who do good to you, what reward will you have? For even sinners do the same. And if you greet only your brethren, what more are you doing than the others? Do not even the tax collectors do so? (Chap. 25:15)

Christ explains, corrects
and deepens the word:

Therefore, accept and receive your neighbor in your heart, even if he does not love you, even when he does not help you and ignores you, by refusing to greet you. Do love him! Do help him selflessly and greet him – even if it is only in thought, when he does not wish to be greeted with words. A greeting from the heart, which is given in thought, also enters the soul and brings good fruit at the right time.

Make sure that you act like the sun that gives – whether the person wants to see it or not, whether he wishes for rain or storm, whether he wants the cold or the warmth.

Give selfless love, as the sun gives to the earth, and respect all people, all Being. Then you will receive your reward in heaven.

Do not say what people want to hear. Do not discriminate, like people who associate only with those who think and act the same way and condemn those who think and act otherwise.

Do Not Tie Yourselves to People or Things

16. And if you desire something as much as your life, but it leads you away from the truth, let go of it, for it is better to enter life possessing the truth than to lose life and be cast into outer darkness. (Chap. 25:16)

Christ explains, corrects
and deepens the word:

What the person craves for himself personally concerns his person, his base ego. All this is binding. A binding means to be tied to people and things. The one who ties himself to people and things, that is, who is bound to something, reduces the flow of cosmic energies.

If you tie a person to yourself solely for the sake of having an advantage, then, with your self-will, you pursue interests which lead you away from the life in Me, the Christ. You thereby forsake the impersonal selfless life; you entangle yourself in wanting to possess, to be and to have, and impoverish the spiritual life in your inner being. If you do not desist in time from wanting to possess, to be and to have, you will lose everything one day.

If you do not recognize yourself in the effects – for example, through the loss of all your worldly goods or in illness, in misery and in suffering – and do not repent and make amends either, you will wander in the darkness as soul and as human being, because you were intent only on yourself, on your own personal well-being.

Therefore, recognize yourself each day anew, and actualize the laws of God on a daily basis, and give up wishing for something for the sake of your personal ego. Remain truthful – and thus, faithful to the law of God. Then you will enter the life that is your true being – and you will be rich in yourself, because you have opened heaven within you.

The truth that is impersonal cannot flow into a person who is not a vessel of the truth. Such a person is concerned only about himself and accumulates things only for himself. This behavior leads to his turning away from God's eternally flowing power and toward the life of a "stagnant pool": Only what is against the law flows into the pool and little flows out. This means that he will feel on his own body what he has accumulated in his stagnant pool.

On the other hand, the eternal truth flows into and through the person who is a vessel of the truth. He receives from God and gives from God, thus becoming the wellspring of life for many. The cosmic energy of life, the source of all Being, flows through all forms of Being and through those people and souls who have turned toward God, that is, who have become the vessel of God.

Recognize: The eternally streaming power flows only through the person and the soul who do not accumulate for selfish purposes, but give selflessly. Only through the one who gives selflessly does the stream of God flow unceasingly! If God can flow unhindered through a person, then this person lives in the truth, in God, in the life that lasts eternally. Only such people give from Me, the life, because they are in Me, the life and the truth.

Become Perfect As Your Father in Heaven

17. And if you desire something which causes another pain and sorrow, tear it out of your heart. Only in this way will you attain peace. For it is better to endure sorrow than to inflict it on those who are weaker than you.

18. Be therefore perfect, as your Father in heaven is perfect. (Chap. 25:17-18)

Christ explains, corrects and deepens the word:

Everything that goes out from you and is not divine – like unlawful thoughts, words and deeds – can cause pain and sorrow not only to your neighbor, but also to you, yourself. For what the person sows, he will reap.

The harvest corresponds to the seed. It is always harvested by the one who has sown – not by his neighbor. Your neighbor did not sow your seed, and neither will he reap your harvest.

However, your seeds can have wings – like the seeds of different types of flowers, which, after blooming, are carried away by the wind and take root wherever they are able to take hold. So can your thoughts, words and deeds also fall like winged seeds on the field of your neighbor's soul and sprout, if they find the same or similar conditions there.

The same or similar thing to what is in you is also in him, if he becomes upset and angry by the words and deeds with which you caused him sorrow. Stimulated by your winged seeds, he thinks, speaks and does the same or similar thing. You, however, have triggered it and can be called to account for this in the law of sowing and reaping. You are commanded to love your neighbor selflessly and to serve and help him – and not to cause him pain and sorrow by your behavior.

If your neighbor then burdens himself because of your unlawful behavior, because you intruded on the field of his soul and brought causes into vibration, which he later has to bear and from which he has to greatly suffer, then you are bound to him. And if he, too, reacts unlawfully to your behavior, he is, in turn, bound to you. In this or another form of existence, you will have to clear this up together.

Recognize: A small insignificant winged seed of human ego can create a great cause, which already bears its effect in itself.

So, recognize that every cause must be remedied!

Another example: If you send out your negative thoughts, words and deeds like winged seeds and your neighbor hears what you say about him but takes no notice of it, because he has no correspondence to it in the field of his soul, then only you will burden yourself; and you are bound to him – not he to you. Your neighbor can enter heaven because he has not accepted and absorbed your negative seeds, since he did not think or speak in same or similar way. However, if by your wrong behavior you have set causes into motion in your neighbor that would not have had to come into effect in him, because he would have been able to clear them up later without pain and sorrow, then you are the one who bears the greater guilt and has to bear that part which you have caused to your neighbor.

If, therefore, you have to endure pain and sorrow, do not blame your neighbor for your condition. You are the creator of it yourself – and not your neighbor. Your pain and your sorrow are the seeds in your soul that have sprouted and show themselves in or on your body as harvest.

Only I, Christ, your Redeemer, can free you from this – and only when you repent and no longer do the same or similar thing. Then the burden is taken from your soul and it will go better for you.

Recognize: The one who recognizes his pain and his sorrow as his own seed and accepts his suffering shows true inner greatness. This is a sign of spiritual growth; spiritual growth gradually leads to perfection.

The pure being is perfect; it is the image of the Father-Mother-God. It lives in God, and God lives through the pure being.

Blessed are those who are pure in heart; for they will behold God – because they have again become images of the heavenly Father. From a pure, meek heart, flows gentleness and humility.

Walk the Path Within

1. Take heed that you do not give your alms before people, in order to be seen by them. Otherwise you have no reward from your Father in heaven. When you give alms, you should not sound a trumpet before you, as the hypocrites do in the synagogues and in the streets, so that they may be praised by the people. Verily, I say to you, they already have their reward.

2. But when you give alms, do not let your left hand know what your right hand is doing, so that your alms remain secret; and the One who sees into the secret will publicly acknowledge it. (Chap. 26:1-2)

Christ explains, corrects
and deepens the word:

The Sermon on the Mount, lived, is the Inner Path to the heart of God. What a person does not do selflessly, he does for himself. Selflessness is the love for God. Self-interest is human love. The one who does good for his neighbor only when the latter thanks him for it and praises his good deeds has not done it for his neighbor, but for himself. The gratitude and the praise are then his reward. He is thus already rewarded and will receive no further reward from God. Only selflessness will be rewarded by God. Selflessness grows and matures only in the person who has taken the first steps toward the kingdom of the inner being, that is, who has actualized.

The first steps toward this are to monitor and control one's thoughts: Replace egocentric, negative, brooding or passionate thoughts with positive, helpful, joyful, noble thoughts and with thoughts about the good in a person and in all that you encounter. Then you will gradually bring your senses under control. You will then also no longer want anything from your neighbor and will no longer expect anything from him. In the further course of the Inner Path, you will speak only what is positive and essential. Thereby, you gain control over your human ego because you have learned to rest in yourself. Then your soul becomes more and more light-filled and you find in everything that comes toward you the good that you are then able to address and express in the right way. If you have learned this, then you will also address negative matters lawfully. In this way, uprightness and honesty awaken in you and you remain faithful to God in all things.

This spiritual evolutionary process toward selflessness is the Inner Path to the heart of God. Everything that you do out of selflessness brings you manifold fruits.

So, if your sensations are without expectations and your thoughts are noble and good, then the power of God is in your words and in your deeds. This power is My energy of life. It goes into the soul of your neighbor and causes your neighbor to also become selfless. For, sooner or later, what goes out of your light-filled soul will enter your neighbor's soul and his disposition, as well, depending on when he opens himself for it.

The one who gives selflessly does not ask whether his neighbor knows what he has given. The selfless one gives! He knows that God, the eternal Father, sees into the heart of all His children and that the Eternal, whose Spirit dwells in every human being, rewards the selfless one when the time for this has come. This alone is important.

Recognize: All good works, that is, selfless ones, become manifest in the right time, so that those who should see them may recognize them, so that they, too, become selfless, by accepting and striving for the life in Me, and doing what I have commanded them: to love one another selflessly, as I, the Christ, love them.

Learn True Prayer

3. And when you pray, you should not be like the hypocrites who like to pray in the synagogues and on the corners of the streets, so that they may be seen by the people. Verily, I say to you, they already have their reward.

4. But when you pray, go into your chamber and when you have shut the door, pray to your heavenly Father who is hidden away; and the hidden One, who sees into that which is hidden, will publicly acknowledge it. (Chap. 26:3-4)

Christ explains, corrects
and deepens the word:

When you pray, withdraw into a quiet chamber and immerse deeply into your inner being; for the Spirit of the Father, whose temple you are, dwells in you.

If you pray just to be seen or so that your neighbor may think you are pious and devout, then I say to you that this is not devoutness, but false piety; it is hypocrisy. Such externalized prayers are without power. The one who prays just from his lips or to be seen sins against the Holy Spirit, for he misuses holy words for his own self-interest.

Recognize that: If you address God in prayer and do not fulfill in your life what you have prayed for, that is, if your prayers are only a display of your ego and do not come from the depths of your soul and are not inspired by the love for God, then you sin against the Holy Spirit. This is the greatest sin.

When your prayers do not flow selflessly from your heart, it would be better not to pray and to first become aware of your thoughts and human desires and to gradually give them over to Me – so that the selfless love that is in you will grow and you will be able to pray from the heart. Then your prayers will be gradually inspired and imbued by the love for God and for your neighbor.

"... and the hidden One, who sees into what is hidden, will publicly acknowledge it" means that your thoughts of light and your power-filled prayers, which are inspired by the love for God, will still bear fruit in this world. You will be allowed to recognize your seed of love and many will also recognize you as a source of love.

Find the Truth Within You

5. And when you pray together, do not use empty repetitions, as the heathens do; for they think that they will be heard when they make many words. Therefore, you should not do the same as they; for your Father in heaven knows what you need before you ask ... (Chap. 26:5)

Christ explains, corrects
and deepens the word:

Only the person who has actualized very little of the law of truth uses many words and empty, uninspired repetitions in prayer and in daily life.

The one who speaks a lot about the law of truth and of life, thus using many words for it, cannot fill them with power and life, because he is not himself filled with the law of God. Such words are egocentric and, for that reason, without love, although chosen as if they were carried by love. A speech that is not inspired by the soul does not reach the innermost recesses of your neighbor's soul, and thus finds no echo in the person who lets the love of God prevail in and through him. The one who speaks without inspiration about the law of truth and of life, which, however, he himself does not actualize, merely stimulates a person, who hears this and likewise is still oriented to outer things, to engage in arguing.

Recognize that a person who argues about spiritual principles of the law does not know the laws of God. Everyone who wants to argue is convinced that he knows better than his neighbor and wants to confirm this to himself. The one who argues only gives evidence of himself, namely, that he knows nothing and is unsure. This is why he argues.

However, the one who has found the truth does not argue about the truth, not even about what belief is. The word "belief" also implies a lack of knowledge: In the end, the person believes what he does not know or cannot prove. The one who believes in the truth has not yet found the eternal truth. Nor does he move yet in the stream of the eternal truth. Therefore, belief is still blindness.

However, the one who has found the eternal truth no longer has to believe in the truth – he knows the truth, because he moves in the stream of truth. This is the true wise man, who has raised the treasure of truth in himself. The truly wise rest in themselves. This is inner confidence and stability. They do not argue about belief, because they have found their way from belief to wisdom, which is the truth.

Therefore, the one who merely believes in God without knowing the depth of the eternal truth, the eternal law, uses many words about his belief.

Even in prayer, he will behave in a similar way: He uses many words, because he does not inspire his words with selfless love. He is of the opinion that with many words he is able to convince God or even persuade Him. He thinks he has to make himself understood by God, because he assumes that God could understand his prayers differently than what he meant. Pagans think and pray similarly.

Recognize: The deeper the person immerses into the divine wisdom, the fewer words he will use in prayer. His prayers are short yet powerful, because the word radiates the power that is lived.

Actualize Your Prayers

... Therefore, when you are gathered together you should pray in this manner:

6. Our Father, who are in heaven, hallowed be Your name. Your kingdom come. Your will be done on earth, as it is in heaven. Give us day by day our daily bread and the fruit of the living vine. And as You forgive us our sins, so may we also forgive the sins of others. Leave us not in temptation. Deliver us from evil. For Yours is the kingdom and the power and the glory in all eternity. Amen. (Chap. 26:5-6)

Christ explains, corrects
and deepens the word:

The community prayer, the Lord's Prayer, is prayed with different words and contents, because every community prays it according to the potential of love of the community.

As Jesus of Nazareth, I taught the community prayer, the Lord's Prayer, in My mother tongue, that is, with other words, and thus with another content than was prayed in later times and in other languages.

The words as such are unessential. What is important is that the person actualize what he prays. Then every word that comes out of his mouth is inspired with love, power and wisdom.

You should not pray according to the letter nor strive to pray, word for word, the Lord's Prayer, which I taught My own. What is essential is that you inspire the words of your prayers with the love for the Eternal and for your neighbor, and that the content of your prayers correspond to your life.

People who are filled by the eternal truth, the love and wisdom of God, will, in turn, pray in another way than those who pray only because it was thus taught to them or because they belong to a denomination where the prayers are spoken according to the consciousness of the denomination.

People who are on the path to their divine origin pray freely, that is, with self-chosen words that are inspired by love and power.

People who live in My Spirit, who are imbued with the love and wisdom of God, who thus actualize the laws of God in their daily life will, above all, thank God for their life and for everything. They will praise and glorify Him and devote their life more and more to Him – in sensations, thoughts, words and deeds – because they have become life of His life.

People in the spirit of the Lord live their prayer. This means that they fulfill the laws of the Eternal more and more, and have themselves become the prayer, which is an adoration of God.

Therefore, the one who fulfills the will of God lives in adoration of God more and more. Such people not only keep the laws of God, but they have become the law of love and wisdom, for the most part.

In the growing Kingdom of Peace of Jesus Christ that is unfolding, in which I Am the ruler and the life, the people will keep the law of God more and more. Many of them will have become the law – and thus, God-men who personify the life, God, in all that they think, speak and do. Their prayers are the life in Me, the fulfillment of the eternal law. With their life, which is the law of God, they give thanks to God for the life.

And so, gratitude to God is the life in God. Their life, which is a single act of giving thanks, streams into the Kingdom of Peace.

They pray according to the following words, which they fulfill in daily life:

Our Father, Your Spirit is in us,
and we are in Your Spirit.
Hallowed is Your eternal name in us
and through us.
You are the Spirit of life;
You are our Ur-Father.
We bear our eternal names from you.
You, eternal One, have given them to us
and have placed in our names the whole
fullness of infinity.
Our names, which You have breathed into us,
are the love and wisdom –
the fullness out of You,
the law in us and through us.
Our eternal kingdom is the infinity –
the power and the glory, in and from You.
We are heirs to the eternal kingdom.
Therefore, we are the kingdom itself,
the eternal homeland.
It is in us and is effective through us.
Your infinite, glorious will is in us
and is effective through us.
The power of Your will is our strength of will.

It is effective in us and through us,
for we are spirit of Your Spirit.
Heaven is not space and time –
heaven and earth are one,
because we are united in You.
The love and power in and through us
is our daily bread.
You, O eternal, glorious Father,
have brought forth in us all
that vibrates in infinity.
Through us, You create
in heaven and on earth.
We are in You, and You prevail
in us and through us.
We are filled in Your Spirit,
for we are spirit
of Your Spirit.
In you we are rich
for we live our heritage,
infinity out of You.
Our eternal heritage,
spirit of Your Spirit,
brings forth all that we need
as human beings in the Kingdom of Peace.
We live in You and from You.
Life streams and gives itself.
We live in the fullness of God,
because we are ourselves the fullness.
The earth is heaven

and the Kingdom of Peace
is the richness of the earth,
in which we live and are –
spirit of Your Spirit.
We live in the inner kingdom –
and yet are human beings who personify
externally that which radiates in the inner being.
Praised is the name of the Lord;
He is the life in and through us.
The name of God is the law of love
and of freedom that is lived.
Sin is transformed –
the light is come.
We live from His light
and live in and from His Spirit,
for we are spirit of His Spirit.
In God everything has been cleared.
His name has made everything pure.
The glory of God be praised!
God's will, love and wisdom
permeate the earth and the land.
We are ourselves earth and land –
will, love and wisdom.
In us is the kindness of God –
the good from God.
We are in God and act from God.
The earth is the Lord's –
it is the kingdom of love.
It is effective in us and through us.

The life, the glory of the Father,
is effective in us and through us –
from eternity to eternity.

In its essence, this glorification is the life of those who live in the Kingdom of Peace of Jesus Christ. They live in Me, the Christ, and I live through them; and together we live in the Father-Mother-God, and the Father lives through us from eternity to eternity.

Find the Positive in the Negative

7. For if you forgive men their trespasses, your heavenly Father will also forgive you. But if you do not forgive men their trespasses, your Father in heaven will not forgive you your trespasses.

8. And when you fast, do not look downcast like the hypocrites. For they disguise their faces, in order to appear as men who fast. Verily, I say to you, they already have their reward.

9. And I say to you, you will never find the Kingdom of Heaven unless you protect yourself from the world and its evil ways. And you will never see the Father in heaven, unless you keep the Sabbath and cease your haste to gather riches. But when you fast, anoint your head and wash your face, so that you do not display yourself before the people with your fasting. And the holy One, who sees into that which is hidden, will publicly acknowledge it. (Chap. 26:7-9)

Christ explains, corrects
and deepens the word:

The commandment to forgive and ask for forgiveness holds true until all that is not in accordance with the eternal laws is atoned for and cleared up. The commandment to forgive and ask for forgiveness is a part of the law of sowing and reaping. It will be revoked when all humanness has been cleared and every soul has become a pure, immaculate spirit being.

So until then, the following commandment holds true: Forgive and you will attain forgiveness. If you ask for forgiveness and your neighbor forgives you, then your Father in heaven has also forgiven you. But if you ask for forgiveness and your neighbor does not forgive you because he is not yet ready to do so, then your eternal Father will not forgive you either. The one who has sinned against his neighbor must also receive forgiveness from his neighbor. Only then will God take away the sin.

The eternally just One loves all His children – including those who do not yet have the strength to forgive. If He were to forgive only the one who caused a sin to be committed without forgiving the one who was led to commit this sin and cannot yet forgive – then where would the justice of God be? Both can enter heaven only when their sins have been cleared up.

For this reason, be careful of what goes out of your mouth and pay attention to your deeds, whether they are in accordance with the eternal law, that is, whether they are selfless! That which is against the law is said or done very quickly – but it can take a long time before it is forgiven.

If you have asked for forgiveness and your neighbor is not yet ready to forgive you, then the grace of God will grow stronger in you; it will envelop you and carry you – however, He will not take away from you what has not yet been cleared up. God's mercy will then also grow stronger in your neighbor and, respecting his free will, will lead him while in such a way that he more promptly recognizes his faults, repents and forgives you. Only when you have been forgiven all those against whom you have sinned – that is, when everything has been cleared up – can you enter heaven, because God will have then transformed all humanness into divine power.

God is omnipresent. Thus, He is also effective in the law of sowing and reaping. And in everything negative is the positive, God, the eternal law. If a person recognizes and repents of his sins and faults, then the positive powers will become active in them and will strengthen the person, who has come to know his guilt, to clear up his sins with Christ's strength.

Recognize the law of God; it is eternal life from eternity to eternity – everything in all things: Everything is contained in everything: the smallest in the large and the large in the smallest, the strength to forgive in the sin, and the ascent to the Inner Life, to the eternal Being, in the power that is set free through forgiveness.

Therefore, the divine can also be effective in the negative when the person asks for forgiveness from his heart, forgives and sins no more. However, the person must take the first step toward the Inner Life.

Recognize that everything you do – be it praying, fasting or giving alms – if you do not do it selflessly, but to be seen by your fellow man, then you have already received your reward from the people. God will not reward you then. And if you fast only because of your corpulence, you will not increase the Spirit of your Father in you. However, the person who takes in nourishment in the name of the Most High and exercises moderation, fasting from time to time, in order to relax and purify his body so that the power of God can maintain all cells and organs in the right way, is the one who sincerely practices accepting and receiving in himself the life from God, in order to live in this life. And at the same time, he will dedicate his life to God, the Eternal, in prayer, in order to gradually become the prayer that is lived.

10. You should do likewise when you mourn for the dead and are sad, for your loss is their gain. Do not act like those who mourn before the people and make loud lamentation and rend their garments, so that others may see their sadness. For all souls are in the hands of God and all those who have done good will rest with their ancestors in the bosom of the Eternal.

11. Pray, rather, for their rest and ascent, and consider that they are in the land of rest, which the Eternal has prepared for them, and will receive just reward for their deeds, and do not murmur like hopeless people. (Chap. 26:10-11)

Christ explains, corrects
and deepens the word:

The one who mourns for the dead is still far from eternal life, because he sees death as the end of life. He has not yet reached the resurrection in Me, the Christ. He is counted among the spiritually dead.

Do not mourn your dead! For the one who mourns the loss of a person does not consider the gain of the soul, which – if it has lived in Me, the Christ – enters into higher consciousness spheres of life. For if its life in its earthly existence was in God, then it will also be in God in another form of existence.

Recognize that the temporal, the life in the body, is not the life of the soul. The soul has taken on flesh for just a short segment of life, in order to clear up and settle in the temporal what it had inflicted upon itself in different earthly garments. The earth is to be seen as a mere transit station where the souls in earthly garment can clear up in brief time what they cannot overcome so quickly beyond the veils of consciousness – also called the walls of fog.

When a soul leaves its earthly garment, a person cries only for the garment of the soul, not thinking of the soul that has slipped out of the garment.

After laying aside its earthly body, a light-filled soul will be led, by light-filled beings invisible to humans, into the plane of consciousness that corresponds to the way of thinking and living of the person in whom this soul was incarnated.

Recognize: Every soul that has left its body is drawn, for some time still, to the people with whom it lived together as a human being. Should it learn that its former earthly relatives mourn for its shell, this is very painful for the soul. The soul that is still close to earth recognizes very well why its relatives grieve only over its human shell and why it is ignored as a soul by the mourners. A soul that has to recognize this then feels the first deep soul-pain after laying aside its physical body; for it learns why the person mourns instead of thinking of it with love and unity. With this, it perceives many a self-serving thought from its former earthly relatives. It cannot draw their attention to itself, because it is not perceived by them. What it says the person does not hear, and what it can see he does not see. But the soul perceives many things.

I suggest you think about this: Do you grieve when the snake sheds its skin, when it leaves its skin behind and slithers away?

It is similar with the soul. It leaves its perishable body, its shell, and journeys on. Therefore, you are grieving the loss of the shell, and are not remembering the soul. The person who remembers the soul thanks God who called the soul back to His bosom, insofar as the soul made use of a life in God while in the earthly garment, thereby drawing closer to Him. Remember that for a light-filled soul, discarding the body is a gain.

And if you mourn the loss of a person just in front of people, you are playing the hypocrite. In reality, you think neither of the person nor of the soul. You think only of yourself. The soul, which registers this, recognizes that it has not been loved selflessly, that perhaps it was there just to serve its neighbor's self-interest.

Many souls have to recognize that, while in the earthly garment, their earthly relatives and acquaintances lived through them. This means that, as human beings, they could not develop themselves and live according to their own characteristics, because they had to do the will of those who demanded of them what was advantageous to the former. Many of these souls perceive what they missed in their earthly existence and, for this reason, return again into the earthly existence. They return to the earth through the veils of consciousness and, as souls, they again stay among those who had lived through them. Still others seek to live on earth those things they were unable to develop as human beings.

As long as people are tied to people or things – like possessions, wealth and power – their souls return to earth and slip again into new earthly garments. There are manifold causes and reasons why souls reincarnate. If a soul recognizes, for example, that it is chained to its relatives through sin, then it often becomes resigned and gives in to the wish to take on a new body. Inspired by this wish, it lives on the plane of consciousness that corresponds to its spiritual state and is taught there. Among other things, it is made to understand the pros and cons of a new incarnation. It then goes into incarnation when the stars – in which its pros and cons are stored and thereby, its pathway to earth – show the way to matter and when an earthly body is conceived on earth that corresponds to its spiritual level of consciousness. It then slips into this human shell at its birth.

The man who begot the body and the woman in whom the embryo grew attracted that soul with which they still have something to clear up, or, in order to walk the path of the Lord together, in selfless service for their neighbor.

The person should not look just to his body, but above all to the incarnated being within him, and should strive to do the will of God and not allow the human will of a second or third person to be imposed on him.

Recognize: Even if you say "I do the will of my neighbor, to keep the outer peace," you prevent your soul and your neighbor's soul as well, from developing and unfolding as it is good for both. You prevent yourself and your neighbor from fulfilling the tasks that your souls have brought along into the earthly existence: to purify itself and to free itself from the burden of sin, which perhaps was brought into this incarnation from previous incarnations. Whoever allows his fellow man to lead him by the nose – doing what others say although he recognizes that this is not his way – is lived and his own actual earthly existence passes him by. He does not use the days; he is used by those to whom he is servile and therefore does not know his own path over this earth as a human being.

The one who binds his fellow man, by forcing his will upon him, is comparable to a vampire that sucks the energy from its fellow man. He does not know himself, and at the same time, he ties himself to his victim, and vice versa; the victim who lets himself be drained also ties himself to the former. Both will be brought together again in one of their lives, either in an earthly garment or as souls in the spheres beyond – and this, so often and for so long, until the one has forgiven the other.

If two people tie themselves to each other – regardless of who does the binding or lets himself be bound – both have burdened themselves and both must clear things up together, so that love and unity can be re-established between them.

No one can say, "I did not know about the laws of life." I say to you that Moses brought you excerpts from the eternal laws, the Ten Commandments. And if you keep these, then you will not tie yourselves to each other, but will live in peace with one another.

Recognize: Only love and unity among one another show souls and people the pathways to the higher life.

God, the eternally kind One, offers His hand to each soul and to each person. The one who takes it uses his earthly life. He treasures the days and is also able to live them according to the commandments, by clearing up what the day shows him. As soul, he will one day walk and rest in God with all those who likewise have used their earthly existence by recognizing and overcoming with Me, the Christ, what the day brought and showed them day after day – joy and suffering.

And if you do not mourn for your own sake the mortal shell that your neighbor discarded, but rejoice in spirit that the soul in earthly garment has recognized its spiritual life and has prepared itself for it, then you will pray joyfully for your neighbor to the Father, through Me, the Christ. You will send forces of love to the soul that is now closer to God, so that it may move on to higher planes in order to unite with God more and more.

The soul feels the joy and suffering of its relatives. The souls that passed away in Me, the Christ, feel linked through Me, the Christ, with all those who still walk in the earthly garment. The joy of the soul for being remembered with love by its relatives fills it with strength.

Recognize: Selfless, loving prayers give power and strength to the soul that journeys on its path toward the divine. In your selfless prayers it feels the caring closeness and receives increased strength. Through this, it will more quickly lay aside the humanness that still clings to it, thus becoming free for Him, who is freedom and love – God, the life. The reward from God is great for every soul that earnestly strives to fulfill the will of God.

Recognize: Only the one who merely speaks about his faith is without hope, but he does not live what he appears to believe. In the last analysis, the doubter does not believe in what he pretends to believe. From this, hopelessness develops.

Where Your Treasure Is, There Is Your Heart

12. You should also not gather for yourselves treasures on earth, which the moths and rust consume and which thieves dig up and steal. But gather for yourselves treasures in heaven, where neither moths nor rust consume them and where thieves neither dig up nor steal. For where your treasure is, there is also your heart.

13. The eyes are the lamps of the body. So if you see clearly, your whole body will be full of light. But if your eyes are lacking or if they are dull, your whole body will be dark. Now if the light that is in you is darkness, how great the darkness will be!

14. No one can serve two masters. Either he will hate the one and love the other, or he will be devoted to the one and despise the other. You cannot serve God and the mammon at the same time. (Chap. 26:12-14)

Christ explains, corrects
and deepens the word:

Only the person who does not believe in God, in His love, wisdom and goodness, collects treasures on earth. Many people pretend to believe in God; however, you will recognize them by their works. Many people talk about the love and the works of God – by their deeds alone, will you recognize them.

Many people talk about the inner kingdom and about the inner wealth, and yet gather in the barns for themselves personally and accumulate worldly riches for themselves personally, so as to be held in high esteem by the people.

The one who is concerned only about his personal well-being does not yet sense the bird of prey that has already raised its wings to destroy the nest and steal the wealth, which the rich man, the builder of the nest, calls his personal property.

However, the one who strives first for the Kingdom of God gathers inner values, inner treasures. He will also receive in the temporal all that he needs and beyond that.

The one who is rich in his inner being will not live in want externally. But the one who is externally rich and hoards his wealth will live in want some day. The one who gathers treasures on earth will find them taken away from him so that he may reflect on the treasure of the inner being and be able to go into the life, into the inner wealth.

The soul will lack divine light for so long until it strives first for the Kingdom of God. And as long as it is still possible on earth, a light-poor soul will again be born into a light-poor body and will perhaps live in poverty among the poor. The recognition will come that the treasure, the wealth, is in God alone.

The one whose heart is with God will be rich in inner values and will enter the Kingdom of Peace.

I, Christ, give you a criterion, so that you may recognize where you stand – either in the light or in the shadow, "For where your treasure is, there is also your heart," and there your soul will be one day.

Take heed: The one who reads these words and stands at the turning-point of the old to the New Era should hasten, so that he may still find his spiritual life! For when the New Era, the era of Christ, is manifest over the whole earth and the Inner Life is lived, incarnations will no longer be possible for those who strive for external values. Then, incarnations will also no longer be possible for the worldly rich, so that as the poorest among the poor they atone for what they neglected to do as the rich.

Once the Kingdom of Peace of Jesus Christ has taken further evolutionary steps, there will be neither poor nor rich. All people will then be rich in My Spirit, for they will have opened the inner kingdom. They will also live accordingly on the new earth, under another heaven.

For this reason, be prepared to serve God and, out of love for God, your fellow man as well.

Recognize: No one can serve two masters, God and mammon. Only selfless love unites all people and nations. Both the human being on earth and the soul in the spheres of purification will one day be led to the decision to serve God or mammon, to be for God or against God. There is nothing in between: either for God, or for the satanic.

Seek First the Kingdom of God

15. Therefore, I say to you: Do not be anxious for your life, what you will eat and drink; not even for your body, for what you will put on. Is not life more than food and the body more than clothing? And what shall it profit a man, if he would gain the whole world but lose his life?

16. Look at the birds in the air: they neither sow nor reap, nor gather into barns, and yet your heavenly Father nourishes them. Are you not cared for much better than they? But who among you could add one cubit to his life span, if he wanted to? And why are you so concerned about your clothing? Consider the lilies of the field, how they grow; they neither toil nor spin. And yet, I say to you, even Solomon in all his splendor and glory was not arrayed like one of these.

17. But if God so clothes the grass of the field, which today is alive and tomorrow is burnt in the oven, should He not much more clothe you, O you men of little faith?

18. Therefore, you should not be anxious and ask: What will we eat? What will we drink? Or: What will we wear? (As the Gentiles do.) For your heavenly Father knows that you need all that. But seek first the Kingdom of God and His righteousness, and all these things will be added to you. Therefore, do not be concerned about the evil of tomorrow. It is enough that each day has its own evil. (Chap. 26:15-18)

Christ explains, corrects
and deepens the word:

The person who worries about his personal life, about his well-being – for example, what he will eat and drink or clothe himself with tomorrow – is a poor planner; because in so doing, he thinks only of himself, of his own well-being and of his possessions. With this, he also plans in his pain and woe at the same time.

On the other hand, the one who fulfills the will of God is a good planner. He will plan both his days and his future. However, he knows that his planning is only a projection that rests in the hands of God.

He puts his plan in the hands of God and works with the powers of God, letting himself be guided by God during the events of the day. For he knows that God is the all-knowing Spirit and the wealth of his soul. The person who entrusts himself to God, who places his day's work into the light of God and fulfills the law "pray and work" will receive his just reward. He will have everything that he needs.

If God, the Eternal, adorns nature and clothes the lilies of the field, how much more will He feed and clothe His child who fulfills His will! Therefore, do not worry about tomorrow, but plan and commit your plan to the will of God – and God, who knows your plan, will fulfill what is good for you.

I give you an example: A good architect will carefully plan a house and pay attention to all the details.

Once he has finished his plan, he will check it again and will then submit it to be looked over by the client who commissioned the building. If the latter agrees to the plan, then the workmen will work according to it. The architect and his client will supervise the execution of the plan and will interfere only when something does not conform to the planning.

You should lead your life in a similar way. Plan each day and plan well! Allow yourselves time for some hours of reflection, too, in which you can find the inner stillness to think over your life and your planning again and again. With His will, God will also penetrate a carefully made plan of the day that has been placed in His will. The one who carries out his plan in this way need not worry about tomorrow. His belief in the guidance of God consists of positive thoughts; from these emerge positive words and law-abiding actions. Positive thoughts, words and actions are the best tools, because the will of God is active in them. This means that the will of God, His Spirit, is at work in every positive thought, in every selfless word, in every selfless gesture and deed. God will give the good planner all that he needs and beyond that.

Only the one who does not entrust himself to God, who lets the days slip by and does not use them, worries about tomorrow. The person who lives from day to day and then blames his neighbor when he fails in many things, when he is sick, when he goes hungry, when he cannot acquire what he needs for his daily life – is not a good planner. He is an anxious and egocentric person who attracts what he does not want and what he fears. The person who does not plan the hours, days and months with God's help and does not place his plan and himself in the will of God cannot be guided by God. Only the one who entrusts his daily work to God and conscientiously fulfills the commandment "pray and work" can be guided by God and is filled by Him – he is filled with love, wisdom and power. This means that his vessel, his life, is filled with trust and faith in God.

People in the Spirit of God will not live in want. They are good planners, they are strong in faith and work with the powers of the Spirit. Only the anxious person is concerned about himself, about his small ego. He worries about tomorrow, because he is not secure in God and does not believe in God's wisdom and love. With this, he unconsciously opens the barn for the thieves who come and steal. He will lose what he has seized and hoarded for himself personally.

From the hands of God, people receive food, shelter and clothing. The one who places his life, his thinking and his work in the hands of God need not worry about tomorrow. He will have what he needs today, tomorrow and in the future – and beyond that.

And so, whoever lives in the inner kingdom will not live externally in want, either. However, the one who is poor in his inner being will live externally in want. If today he lives externally and increases worldly wealth for himself, keeping it for himself personally, then he is poor in his inner being and will live in want in another earthly garment, that is, he will be poor.

Therefore, strive first for the Kingdom of God and His justice, then God will give you everything you need and beyond that. Look at the birds of the air. They neither sow nor reap, nor gather into barns; and yet, your heavenly Father feeds them. "Consider the lilies of the field, how they grow; they neither toil nor spin." Nature in all its diversity is clad more beautifully than the richest of the rich. The one who thinks only about his well-being and his full barns will earn his bread by the sweat of his brow, either in this earthly existence or in another incarnation – as long as this is still possible.

The right"pray and work" means to work for oneself and for the common good. Recognize: The lilies of the field – all of nature – are there for all people and give themselves to them in the most manifold ways. The one who is able to understand and appreciate this will not have to earn his bread by the sweat of his brow. He will fulfill the law "pray and work" – for himself and for his neighbor.

And if it is written "they neither toil nor spin," this means that a person should not think solely of himself and work only to gain profit for himself alone, so as to adorn and display himself with it.

Recognize: All Being is in the care of God. Animals, trees, plants, grasses and stones are in the care of God.

They are in the midst of an evolutionary life that is guided by the eternal Creator-God. Since all life comes from God, the animals, trees, plants, grasses and stones also sense and feel. They experience in themselves the evolutionary force of the Creator that invigorates them and leads them to further unfoldment in the cycle of divine aeons. The Creator-power, the eternal Being, gives the nature kingdoms what they need. The gifts of life flow to the life forms to the same extent as these have spiritually unfolded.

The eternal Father remembers every blade of grass. How much more does the Eternal remember His children who have already unfolded in themselves the evolutionary steps of the mineral, plant and animal kingdoms! The children of God bear in themselves the microcosm from the macrocosm and are thus in communication with all of infinity.

But how poor is the person who worries about tomorrow! He shows that he has not yet come to terms with yesterday, since he is unable to live in today, in the now, that is, in God.

The inner being of a person, the pure Being, is the quintessence of infinity. Whoever grasps this as a human being looks to within and unfolds the laws of life, so that he is able to see all things external in the light of truth.

Recognize: Infinity serves the person who thinks and lives in an all-encompassing, that is, unlimited, way.

People in the spirit of love are not self-centered, but all-conscious. They are in constant communication with the forces of God in all Being. Whatever they do, they do from within, with the power of love. They plan and work according to the commandment "pray and work" and do not waste the day. They know the inestimable value of the day, the hours and the minutes, and make use of the time.

Therefore, the one who truly lives does not worry about tomorrow; already today, he receives what he will have tomorrow. For the one who lives in God will not be in want, neither today nor tomorrow. But the one who stays anxious and clings to his belongings will be poor tomorrow.

However, the one who sees himself as a cosmic being, who fulfills the will of God without reservation, attains wisdom and strength. The life of the person who is filled with love and wisdom is permeated with the power of God. He will lack nothing. But whoever worries about tomorrow and sees a gloomy future attracts evil; and he will have his burden every day.

And so, do not think anxiously about tomorrow! Plan with God's strength – and let the Eternal be effective through you. Then your thoughts are positive magnets that attract, in turn, what is positive and constructive. For thoughts, words and deeds are magnets. According to their kind, they attract, in turn, the same or like thing.

Do Not Judge Your Neighbor

1. Do not judge, that you will not be judged. For you will be judged as you judge others; and with whatever measure you measure, you will, in turn, be measured. And as you do to others, so will it be done to you. (Chap. 27:1)

Christ explains, corrects
and deepens the word:

You have read that thoughts, words and deeds are magnets. The one who judges and condemns his neighbor in thoughts and with words will experience the same or like things on himself.

Recognize that your negative thoughts, words and deeds are your own judges. "With whatever measure you measure" – whether in thoughts or in words and actions – so will you yourself be measured. Just as you denigrate your neighbor, in order to exalt yourself, so will you be evaluated: You will know and suffer your own worth.

And if you say "What the one has is enough for him – the other one should receive more," then one day you will possess only as much or even less than the one to whom you have conceded less. Just as you treat your neighbor in thoughts, words and deeds, so will you fare yourself one day.

2. How is it that you see the splinter in your brother's eye and are not aware of the beam in your own eye? Or how can you say to your brother that you want to take the splinter out of his eye? And see, a beam is in your eye. You hypocrite, first take the beam out of your own eye; only then will you see clearly, in order to be able to take the splinter out of your brother's eye. (Chap. 27:2)

Christ explains, corrects
and deepens the word:

Only the person who is not aware of the beam in his own eye talks constantly about the splinter in the eye of his neighbor. Only the one who does not know his own thinking and living busies himself with wanting to extricate the splinter from the eye of his brother. Whoever does not know himself or his beam – the sins of his soul that are reflected in his own eyes – has no eye for the truth. His eye is clouded by sin. He then sees in his neighbor only what he himself still is: a sinner. Only the one who works on the beam in his own eye sees increasingly more clearly. Then, he will be able to recognize the splinter in his brother's eye ever more clearly and will help him remove it, according to the law of love of neighbor.

And so, whoever speaks negatively about his fellow man, who denigrates and slanders him, does not know his own faults.

You shall recognize them by their fruits! Each one shows who he is, himself, that is, his fruit. Whoever gets upset about his fellow man and makes fun of him shows who he truly is.

The one who first discards his own faults is also able to help his neighbor. This is why every one who speaks disparagingly about his brother's faults – and in so doing does not notice the beam in his own eye – is a hypocrite.

Do Not Proselytize

3. You should not give what is holy to the dogs nor cast your pearls before the swine, lest they trample them with their feet, turn round and rend you. (Chap. 27:3)

Christ explains, corrects
and deepens the word:

It is not in accordance with the eternal law of free will that you go with the words of truth from place to place, from house to house, using your skills to persuade and convince, proselytizing to every one you get hold of. For that would mean that you do not hold the truth sacred, and do as it is figuratively written, "You should not give what is holy to the dogs nor cast your pearls before the swine." This means, you should not force the word of God on your neighbor. The one who thinks his neighbor should believe and accept what he thinks he is convinced of still has doubt himself and questions his own belief.

To proselytize means to want to convince. Who ever wants to convince is himself not convinced in his own inner being of what he extols.

However, be good role models in your belief and not those who proselytize. You can offer the body of your belief and leave everyone the option, to believe in it or not, to go along with you or not.

The freedom in God is an aspect of the eternal law. If your neighbor approaches you of his own free will and asks you about your belief, he is taking the first step toward you; and the one who is firm in his belief will then go toward his neighbor and answer him.

Whoever is linked with his neighbor in a divine way will not tie him to his belief – but will share with him only as much as he himself has recognized and actualized. Only the person who has developed little selfless love will want to tie his neighbor to his belief.

For this reason, beware of the overly zealous, who want to convince you of their belief. Offer the eternal truth in the spoken and written word – and live accordingly yourselves; then, those who have recognized the life in themselves will come to you.

Go Into Your Inner Being

4. Ask, and it will be given to you; seek, and you will find. Knock, and it will be opened to you; for every one who asks will receive and the one who seeks will find, and to those who knock it will be opened. (Chap. 27:4)

Christ explains, corrects
and deepens the word:

Only the person who has not yet entered his inner being, the kingdom of love, asks, seeks and knocks at the gate to Inner Life. The Kingdom of God is within, in the soul of every person.

The first step on the path to Inner Life, on the pathway to the gate of salvation, is to ask God for help and support. The next step is to search for the love and justice of God. The pilgrim finds the life, God's love and justice, in the commandments of life, which are the guides on the way within.

A further step is to knock at the inner door, in one's own little chamber of the heart. This gateway to the heart of God opens itself only to the one who has sincerely prayed, searched and knocked. The inner door does not open to the intellectual who seeks only external values and ideals. And the doubters will not be received either.

Therefore, the one who asks, seeks and knocks must do so out of love for God and not to test the love of God.

Recognize that whoever just wants to test whether God's love actually exists will himself be put to the test very quickly. The heart's gateway stands open to the one who lives in God. He need not ask anymore; he has already received, for God knows His children. The one who has entered the heart of God has already received in his soul. This means that the wealth from God shines more intensely in his soul and radiates through him, the person. Whoever has entered his inner being no longer needs to seek – he is at home in the kingdom of the inner being. And whoever has consciously taken up dwelling in Him no longer needs to knock; he has already entered and lives in God, and God lives through him.

Only those will ask, seek and knock who still stand on the outside and do not yet know that, deep in their soul, they bear what makes them truly rich: God's love and wisdom.

Give What You Expect

5. Which man among you here gives a stone when his child asks for bread, or a serpent when he asks for a fish? If you, who are evil, can nevertheless give good gifts to your children, how much more will your Father in heaven give good things to those who ask Him.

6. Whatever you want that people should do to you, do it likewise to them, and whatever you do not want them to do to you, do not do it to them either; for this is the law and the prophets. (Chap. 27:5-6)

Christ explains, corrects
and deepens the word:

Recognize that you should not demand from your fellow man what you are not willing to give yourself.

If you expect your neighbor to do something for you, ask yourself the question: Why don't you do it yourself? The person, for example, who expects money and property from his neighbor so that, in his laziness, he does not have to work himself, or the person who expects faithfulness from his neighbor while he is not faithful himself, or the person who wants to be accepted and received by his neighbor, yet neither accepts nor receives his fellow man – such a person is selfish and poor in spirit.

Whatsoever you demand of your neighbor is what you do not have in your heart yourself.

It is unlawful to force, from an attitude of expectation, your fellow man into actions, statements or certain behaviors, which, of yourself, you would not be willing to do.

If, in wanting something from your neighbor, you have recognized your expectant attitude, turn back quickly and do first what you would demand of your neighbor.

All coercion is the application of pressure, which produces, in turn, coercion and counter-pressure. Through such extortionary behavior toward your fellow man, you bind yourself to him and turn yourself – as well as the one who lets himself be blackmailed – into a slave of a base nature. Coercive methods such as "I expect of you and you expect of me" or "Each gives to the other what the other demands of the former" lead to binding.

What is bound has no place in heaven. Both who are bound to one another will meet again one day, either in a fine-material life or in further incarnations.

This form of binding does not apply to the workplace. When, in your professional life, you have freely taken a position in a certain field of work and the responsible person gives you duties that you should carry out within the framework of your job, you have given your consent to that upon joining the company. You have freely taken your place in the field of work and on the work team, in order to do what is assigned to you. So, when you choose a job, you should also carry out what is assigned to you, according to the field of work you have chosen yourself. The statement "Whatever you want people to do to you, do it likewise to them ..." therefore, does not apply to a self-chosen profession or field of work.

"Whatever you do not want them [the people] to do to you, do not do it to them either" means: If you do not want to be laughed at and ridiculed, or you do not want to be robbed or lied to, or you do not want to be deprived of your belongings, or you do not want to be led by the nose, or you do not want to be robbed of your free will, or you do not want to be beaten or insulted, then do not do it to your fellow man. For what you do to the least of your brothers, this you do to Me – and to yourself. What you do not want to be done to you, you should not do to any of your neighbors either – for everything that goes out from you returns to you. For this reason, examine your thoughts and guard your tongue!

Resist Temptation – Decide for God

7. Enter by the strait gate. For narrow is the way and strait is the gate that leads to life, and few are those who find it. But wide is the gate and broad is the way that leads to ruin, and there are many who walk on it. (Chap. 27:7)

Christ explains, corrects
and deepens the word:

"... narrow is the way and strait is the gate that leads to life" means that in each one who endeavors to walk the narrow path to life the darkling makes itself known and shows him – as it showed Me, as Jesus of Nazareth

– the treasures and comforts of this world. Each day anew, the satanic should be resisted and opposed. Whoever is not watchful will be servile to it.

Recognize that every person who takes the first steps toward life at first feels confined and restricted, until he has made a final decision. For what he thought and did in human terms until now, he should now cease to do.

The first steps lead into the unknown – they are called belief and trust. Until the first steps are taken, the path to life is strait and narrow. The first hurdles that should be overcome on the path to the heart of God are called: Change your way of thinking and cease your old human habits! Repent, forgive, ask for forgiveness and sin no more! For every individual this means a personal effort and a readjustment of everything that until now was customary to him.

However, the one who perseveres with My strength will leave the narrow path and reach the great road of light into the kingdom of the inner being, on which he will strive toward the gateway into absoluteness, into the life in God, with those who journey into the light.

The person is tested each day: for or against God.

The one who decides against Me, by keeping all human comforts and everything that makes him human, will not be led into temptation on the wide dark road, since he has given himself up to the tempter. Many, indeed, follow this road to ruin. They are not tested like those who walk the narrow path to life.

The one who has given himself up to the tempter thereby also gives his unrestricted assent to what he has to harvest on account of his seed.

You Will Recognize Them by Their Fruit

8. Beware of false prophets, who come to you in sheep's clothing, but inwardly are ravening wolves. You will know them by their fruits. Can one gather grapes from thorns or figs from thistles?

9. Likewise, every good tree brings forth good fruit, but a bad tree brings forth bad fruit. Every tree that does not bring forth good fruit is only fit to be cut down and thrown into the fire. This is why you should distinguish the good from the bad by their fruits.
(Chap. 27:8-9)

Christ explains, corrects
and deepens the word:

At the end of the days of materialism, of the "time of avarice and greed," many false prophets will appear. They will talk a lot about the love of God – and yet their works will be the works of men. Not the one who speaks of the love of God is a true prophet and a spiritually wise man, but solely the one whose works are good.

The gift of discernment, however, is given only to the one who first examines his own cast of mind: whether he truly believes in the gospel of selfless love himself and fulfills what is meant by it, and what he has already actualized himself, out of selfless love toward his neighbor.

You can recognize your fellow man and sense the difference between the good, the less good and the bad, only when you have attained a certain degree of spiritual maturity.

The one who still condemns his neighbor and thinks and speaks negatively about him cannot yet assess his fellow man. He lacks the gift of discernment. He merely passes judgment and does not examine.

If you are still a bad fruit yourself, how can you recognize the good fruit? The one who does not actualize the laws of God thus lacks the gift to discern between what is good, less good and bad.

And so, whoever wants to assess his neighbor should first examine himself to see whether he has the gift of discernment between the just and the unjust.

A good fruit can be discarded very quickly and the bad one approved, when the rotten fruit makes a show of itself with a lot of words, using many seemingly convincing words and gestures.

Recognize: Like attracts like. Rotten fruits are closer than good fruits to the one who is himself still a rotten fruit. But whoever is selfless is a good fruit, and the good, the selfless, is also near him.

Whoever is selfless also has the gift to discern between the good, the less good and the bad fruits. And so, whoever wants to discern between the good and bad fruits must first be a good fruit himself. Only the good fruit can recognize the bad. The bad fruit always seeks like-minded bad fruits, in order to go against the good ones. The bad fruits condemn, reject, judge and bind.

The good, ripe fruits are understanding, of good will and tolerant, and are kind toward their neighbor. They may very well address serious shortcomings, but they keep their neighbor in their heart. This means that they no longer judge, condemn or sentence.

I repeat: You shall recognize them by their fruits.

The good fruit knows the bad fruit, yet the bad fruit does not recognize the good fruit. The good fruit looks only to the good, the bad fruit only to the bad. The person thinks, speaks and acts accordingly.

Fulfill the Will of God

10. Not all who say to Me, Lord! Lord! will enter the Kingdom of Heaven, but those who do the will of My Father who is in heaven. Many will say to Me on that day, Lord, Lord, have we not prophesied in Your name? Have we not cast out devils in Your name? Have we not done many wonderful works in Your name? Then I will declare to them, I have never known you; depart from Me, you evil-doers. (Chap. 27:10)

Christ explains, corrects
and deepens the word:

The one who merely calls on My name and does not fulfill the will of My Father is poor in spirit, despite his seemingly spiritually effective speech and his seemingly courteous words, and will not enter the Kingdom of Heaven.

But the one who accomplishes selfless deeds without expecting reward or acknowledgement is the one who does the will of My Father, for he acts as he thinks and speaks.

Selfless deeds occur only through God-filled sensations and thoughts. If a person's thoughts are impure, then his words are empty and his deeds egocentric.

Recognize that the one who appears to speak from the I Am, that is, who seems to speak My word and appears to accomplish deeds in My name, living well from this, has already received his reward. He will receive no further reward in heaven. The one who does selfless works of love and works for his earthly bread will receive the just reward in heaven.

Recognize that the spiritual bread is the spiritual nourishment for the soul. The bread for the body should be earned according to the law of "pray and work."

The spiritual bread comes from heaven and will be offered to those who keep the law of love and of life and who also fulfill the commandment "pray and work."

God gives human beings material food through the earth. The fruits of the earth require preparation through the work of the hands. Thus, the worker is worthy of his wage.

Recognize the difference between bread for the soul and bread for the earthly body! Both may flow from one source, but the one is spiritual and is offered to the soul, and the other is condensed substance, matter, and is given to the physical body. What the great Spirit, God, gives the people for their physical body requires human work; for example, it must be sown, cultivated, harvested and prepared. For this, the person should also be paid by people.

Only the one who does everything out of love for God and man will be received into the Kingdom of God.

Build on the Rock – Christ

11. Therefore, I compare the one who hears these words of Mine and follows them with a wise man who built his house solidly upon a rock. And the rain fell and the floods came and the winds blew about this house. And it did not fall in, for it was founded upon a rock.

12. And the one who hears these words of Mine and does not follow them should be compared with a foolish man who built his house upon sand. And the rain fell and the floods came and the winds blew and beat against that house and it fell in, and great was its collapse. But a city which is built solidly, walled solidly in a circle or on the top of a hill and founded upon a rock can never fall nor be hidden.

13. And it happened that when Jesus had ended these sayings, the people were astonished at His teaching. For He addressed the head and the heart when He taught and did not speak like the scribes who taught only by the authority of their office. (Chap. 27:11-13)

Christ explains, corrects
and deepens the word:

The one who hears and follows My word develops his spiritual life. He bases his life on Me, the rock. He will then stand firm against all storms and floods. After this earthly life, his soul will consciously enter the spiritual life and will be no stranger there, because while on earth the human being had already lived in the kingdom of the inner being.

The prophetic spirit is the fire in the prophet and in all enlightened ones. God did not and does not speak through them as those "who taught only by the authority of their office." The prophets and enlightened ones spoke and speak with the full authority of the Eternal, the speaking God, whether people want to admit it or not.

It is written, "He addressed the head and the heart." What the intellect, the head, absorbs is talked over and argued by the "head-thinkers." Despite this, many a tiny seed falls into their heart. The one who receives the word of life with his heart also moves it in his heart, causing the good seed, the life, to sprout right away.

But whoever wants to grasp the word of God with his intellect alone will have to later recognize – perhaps only after a few blows of fate – what it is he rejected through his doubt and intellectual arrogance. He will have to recognize that the seed, the word of God that was given from the horn of plenty of life through prophets and enlightened ones, would have spared him much.

The book "This Is My Word" will be in effect into the New Era, into the time of Christ. My life once, as Jesus of Nazareth, and My word as Christ today [1989] are the foundation.

The way I thought, taught and lived as Jesus of Nazareth will be the standard for the way of living and thinking of the people of the New Era in the Kingdom of Peace of Jesus Christ. In this way, I Am very close to them. They will greet Me in the spirit as their brother and will accept and receive Me as the ruler of the Kingdom of God on earth.

This book is a work of love and of life. From it, the people in the Kingdom of Peace will also learn how I initiated and built up the Era of Light on earth. They will learn that I worked through many faithful ones who fought and suffered with Me for the New Era. Therefore, the book "This Is My Word" is a historical document. It will be read now – in the declining old world – as well as then – in the ever more dawning New Era.

The people will also recognize from it the fulfillment of the divine Mission of Redemption, which started with My work as Jesus of Nazareth and then as the Redeemer, as the Christ of God – and now as the builder of the New Era, in which I prepare My coming as the ruler of the Kingdom of Peace, in which I Am brother to those who live in the brotherhood of Christ with Me and with the many whose hearts are pure.

The Twelve Commandments of Jesus

Christianity's Bible contains the Ten Commandments of God, which Moses brought to mankind, and also parts of the teaching of Jesus of Nazareth.

In His work of revelation "This Is My Word, A and Ω, the Gospel of Jesus, the Christ-Revelation that true Christians the world over have come to know," Christ now discloses through the prophetic word all essential aspects of His life on earth and of His teaching which go far beyond the content of the Bible.

In Chap. 46:7-21, we learn that already two thousand years ago Jesus gave the Twelve Commandments to mankind, the commandments for the emerging Kingdom of Peace on this earth. They are a continuation of the Ten Commandments of Moses through Christ, the Son of God, the Redeemer of all men and souls. In this work of revelation it is written:

And Jesus said to them, "Behold, I give you a new law which, however, is not new but old. Just as Moses gave the Ten Commandments to the people of Israel, according to the flesh, so will I give you the twelve commandments for the kingdom of Israel, according to the Holy Spirit.

Who is this Israel of God? All those, from every nation and every tribe, who practice righteousness, love and mercy and who follow My commandments are the true Israel of God." And standing up, Jesus said:

"Hear, O Israel, Jehovah, your God, is the One. I have many seers and prophets. All live and move and have their existence in Me.

You shall not take away the life of any creature for your pleasure or your profit, nor torment it.

You shall not steal the goods of another, nor gather for yourselves more land and riches than you need.

You shall not eat the flesh, nor drink the blood of a slaughtered creature, nor anything else that harms your health or your consciousness.

You shall not make impure marriages, where there is no love and purity, nor corrupt yourself or any creature that has been created pure by the Holy One.

You shall not bear false witness against your neighbor, nor willfully deceive anyone with a lie in order to harm him.

You shall not do to anyone what you do not want to have done to you.

You shall worship the One, the Father in heaven, from whom all things come, and honor His holy name.

You shall honor your fathers and mothers who care for you, as well as all righteous teachers.*

You shall love and protect the weak and oppressed ones and all creatures that suffer wrong.

You shall work all that is good and necessary with your hands. You shall eat the fruits of the earth, so that you live long in the land.

---

* Christ: "to honor" here means as much as "to respect."

You shall cleanse yourselves every day and, on the seventh day, rest from your work, keeping holy the Sabbath and the feasts of your God.

You shall do to others what you want them to do to you."

The Universal Life Series

This Is My Word
A and Ω – The Gospel of Jesus
The Christ-Revelation that true Christians the world over have come to know
1078 pages / Order No. S 007en

This book has NOT been falsified by Jerome or translated by Luther, the enemy of the people. It is from JESUS, the Christ, inspired directly through the prophetic word. A book that gives you knowledge about Jesus, the Christ, about the truth of His activity and life.

The Inner Path - Collective Volume
Levels of Order, Will, Wisdom, Earnestness, And the Great Cosmic Teachings of Jesus....
1341 pages / Order No. S 150en

The main concern of Jesus of Nazareth, and of the Spirit of the Christ of God through His prophetess for today, is the Original Christian School of Life for becoming one with the Spirit of God in us. This is a mystical path of evolution, on which the pilgrim to God opens his spiritual consciousness level by level, thus finding his way to a God-filled life.

Healing by Faith – The Holistic Healing
97 pages / Order No. S 330en

Where Did I Come From? Where Am I Going?
75 pages / Order No. S 407en

The Prophet

The voice of the heart, the eternal truth,
the eternal law of God,
given by the prophetess of God for our time
Fundamental issues of our time
to think about and to serve in self-recognition

No. 1	Founding Figures – Friends or foes of the enterprises they build up
No. 2	Of Priest and Prophets Why have they always been at odds?
No. 3	Who Started It All – Adam or Eve?
No. 4	Building the Divine Work in the Deed – Business management according to the Sermon on the Mount, as received from the Spirit of the Christ of God
No. 5	The Creed of Original Christians
No. 6	Pirouettes of Life Fate, my fate, your fate, our fate, whose life plan? A just or an unjust God?
No. 7	"Christian" living throughout the year. Christmas, the highest celebration of the year?
No. 8	Servile Faith and Its Mysteries
No. 9	The Old-timer and the Prophet
No. 10	The Youth and the Prophet

The voice of the truth ...

Animals Lament – The Prophet Denounces

Human beings torment, abuse and murder their fellow creatures, the animals. In this book, the animals are given a voice that wants to address your heart. It explores the causes for the disdain and indescribable suffering of the animals at the hands of human beings over thousands of years. It also exposes the religious background to this cruelty, while vindicating the prophets of the Old Testament and Christ, who, as Jesus of Nazareth, steadfastly spoke up for the animals.
160 pages, color illustrations, No. 15

The Murder of Animals Is the Death of Humans

Did we humans really believe there would be no consequences for the hundreds of years that we have exploited and polluted our dwelling planet, the Earth, and disdained, tortured and killed God's creatures, the animals, in the cruelest ways possible? Then we have deluded ourselves, for: The cup is full – It is enough! After all the cruelties man has inflicted on the animals and nature, man himself is now on the line. What this means is shown uncompromisingly and clearly in this book.

64 pages, No. 16

The Gabriele Letters

The Gabriele Letters are meant to make alert people aware of how weak in character and schizophrenic our society has become and that the majority of people simply thoughtlessly and numbly accept what the upper ranks of society prescribe.

No. 1, December 2002: Advent and Christmas have become a traditional pagan custom – Why do the animals have to be kept for holiday feasting? – All this has nothing to do with Jesus, the Christ ...

No. 2, January 2003: Highlights on the development of church history – God is not silent. The true God never dwelt in churches of stone – God never blessed weapons – God never let Himself be "represented" by a human being – The true God cannot be bribed ...

No. 3, March 2003: *"The love for God and neighbor and bent, distorted Christianity"* The basis for a peaceable co-existence on Earth – Reincarnation: Original Christian knowledge – Divine justice and the human law

No. 4, July 2003: *"God's Word, the Law of Love and Unity and Those of the Earth Without Rights."* The animal: a wonderful creature from the hand of God; learn to understand the animals – Experiencing the unity of life in nature – Animals want to be friends with us humans, because they know about unity.

The Ten Commandments of God
The Life of the Original Christians
71 pages / Order No. S 504en

Why can't the world, as it is, give us any peace? Because it is not made of selfless love, but of self-love. People have to change their ways be developing the inner love, the selfless love. Then this heard and peaceless world will gradually change. The Ten Commandments show the way, because the are excerpts from the Absolute law of the heavens, from the divine law of selfless love.

The Bible Was Falsified
Jerome, the Church Falsifier of the Bible
45 pages / Order No. S 143en

"Hopelessly corrupted"
" ... in reality no original ever existed, neither a New Testament text nor any bibllical book at all was preserved in its original form. Nor do first copies exist. There are only copies of copies of copies. Today's text of the New Testament is a mixed text, pasted together from various writings that had been passed down. The text of the 'book of books,' today disseminated in more than 100 languages and dialects, is thus hopelessly corrupted."(Church Historian, Karl Heinz Deschner: Abermals krähte der Hahn (Again the Cock Crowed) 1987

Only for the Clever and Analytical Mind:
Who Is Sitting on the Chair of Peter?
Excerpts – 22 pages

Great pagantry, pomp, resplendence and riches are often placed on display at the Holy See. This raises questions: How has the Holy see presented itself in the past? What are its intentions? This book gives answers.

To order any of these books or to obtain a complete catalog of all our books, please contact:

THE WORD
P. O. Box 5643
97006 Würzburg
Germany
or:
Universal Life, the Inner Religion
P. O. Box 3549
Woodbridge, CT 06525
U S A
1-800-846-2691
or:
Universal Life, the Inner Religion
P. O. Box 55133
1800 Shepherd Ave, East
Toronto, ONT M2J 5A0
CANADA
1-800-806-9997

Gabriele Publishing House
P.O. Box 2221, Deering, NH 03244
(844) 576-0937
WhatsApp/Messenger: +49 151 1883 8742
www.Gabriele-Publishing-House.com